Wo...

JEAN
RHYS

Sylvie Maurel

© Sylvie Maurel 1998

First published 1998 by
MACMILLAN PRESS LTD
Houndmills, Basingstoke, Hampshire RG21 6XS
and London
Companies and representatives throughout the world

ISBN 0–333–68393–5 hardcover
ISBN 0–333–68394–3 paperback

A catalogue record for this book is available from the British
Library.

This book is printed on paper suitable for recycling and made from
fully managed and sustained forest sources.

10   9   8   7   6   5   4   3   2   1
07   06   05   04   03   02   01   00   99   98

Typeset by Aarontype Limited,
Easton, Bristol, Great Britain

Printed in Hong Kong

Published in the United States of America 1998 by
ST. MARTIN'S PRESS, INC.,
Scholarly and Reference Division,
175 Fifth Avenue, New York, N.Y. 10010

ISBN 0–312–21687–4

A Irène, Guy et Monique Maurel

Contents

Editors' Preface

The study of women's writing has been long neglected by a male critical establishment both in academic circles and beyond. As a result, many women writers have either been unfairly neglected or have been marginalised in some way, so that their true influence and importance has been ignored. Other women writers have been accepted by male critics and academics, but on terms which seem, to many women readers of this generation, to be false or simplistic. In the past the internal conflicts involved in being a woman in a male-dominated society have been largely ignored by readers of both sexes, and this has affected our reading of women's work. The time has come for a serious reassessment of women's writing in the light of what we understand today.

This series is designed to help in that reassessment.

All the books are written by women because we believe that men's understanding of feminist critique is only, at best, partial. And besides, men have held the floor for quite long enough.

EVA FIGES
ADELE KING

Acknowledgements

My warmest thanks go to Lesley Lawton for her kindness and her patience as editor during the production of the manuscript. I am also deeply grateful to Claire Joubert, who made this project possible.

Abbreviations
and References

ALM   Jean Rhys, *After Leaving Mr Mackenzie* (1930; Harmondsworth: Penguin, 1971)

GMM   Jean Rhys, *Good Morning Midnight* (1939; Harmondsworth: Penguin, 1969)

Q   Jean Rhys, *Quartet* (1928; Harmondsworth: Penguin, 1973)

Sleep   Jean Rhys, *Sleep It Off Lady* (1976; Harmondsworth: Penguin, 1979)

Tigers Jean Rhys, *Tigers Are Better-Looking* (1968; Harmondsworth: Penguin, 1972)

VD   Jean Rhys, *Voyage in the Dark* (1934; Harmondsworth: Penguin, 1969)

WSS   Jean Rhys, *Wide Sargasso Sea* (1966; Harmondsworth: Penguin, 1968)

All page numbers with these abbreviations refer to the Penguin editions of Jean Rhys's works.

1   Introduction

Had Jean Rhys's fiction been merely autobiographical, as so many critics have claimed, her plots would have strained the reader's credulity. Her life was indeed quite out of the ordinary. Jean Rhys was born Ella Gwendoline Rees Williams on 24 August 1890 in Roseau, Dominica, to a Creole mother and a Welsh doctor. She spent her childhood there and left when she was seventeen to attend the Perse School in Cambridge. After a few terms, she decided that she wanted to be an actress and went to the Academy of Dramatic Art in 1909. When her father died suddenly, her family could no longer support her and Jean Rhys found a job in the chorus of a touring company. This is how, as Elgin W. Mellown puts it, 'a young girl from a respectable colonial family [. . .] lived a life that brought her into the demi-mondaine society of pre-War England'.[1]

The cold winters and her fear of the audience having somewhat damped her ardour, she left the tour before long and moved to London, where she had her first love affair with a well-to-do English gentleman twice her age, Lancelot Hugh Smith. The break-up with him was a severe blow to her, and she had an illegal abortion. It was after this traumatic experience that her career branched off. Driven by some uncontrollable impulse which she describes in her autobiography,[2] she wrote an account of the affair in a series of exercise-books which was to cause her to meet Ford Madox Ford and, some twenty years later, provided the basis for *Voyage in the Dark*. Before the First World War, Jean Rhys mostly lived on the allowance which Lancelot Hugh Smith continued to give her long after their affair had ended,

1

but also made a little money of her own, briefly going back to the stage, sitting for artists or getting one or two jobs as a film extra.

During the First World War, she met Jean Lenglet, a Dutchman, joined him in Holland in 1919 and married him. The couple moved to Paris where, in 1920, they had a son who died shortly after birth, then to Vienna, where Jean Lenglet worked as a secretary–interpreter for the Interallied Disarmament Commission. For a year or so, life was sweet and easy as Jean Lenglet was making a lot of money selling foreign currency on the black market, a very profitable business in post-war Austria. In 1921, the Commission moved to Budapest; so did the Lenglets, but soon Jean Lenglet lost the Commission's money and they had to run away to Paris in 1922.

After the luxury hotels of Vienna and Budapest, they were back to square one, finding themselves literally on the streets. In the same year, Jean Rhys gave birth to her second child, Maryvonne. Hunting for money, she tried to sell three of Jean Lenglet's articles which she had translated. As the *Daily Mail* was not interested, she thought of Mrs Adam, then a fairly prominent journalist in Paris, whom she had met before. Mrs Adam asked if Jean Rhys had written anything herself. She reluctantly showed her the exercise-books. Mrs Adam edited them and offered to send the typescript to Ford Madox Ford who, at the time, was publishing young, *avant-garde* writers such as Joyce, Hemingway, Gertrude Stein, Dorothy Richardson and Djuna Barnes. Becoming her patron and then her lover, he encouraged Jean Rhys to write short stories and published 'Vienne' in the last issue of *The Transatlantic Review* in December 1924. In 1923, Jean Lenglet was arrested by the French police, served his sentence and was extradited to Holland where he settled with their daughter. Jean Rhys's first collection of short stories, *The Left Bank*,[3] was published in England with a preface by Ford in 1927, by which time both her marriage and her relationship with Ford were virtually over. She completed *Quartet* and went to England to find a publisher for it; it was initially published as *Postures* in 1928. Between 1928 and 1939, she wrote most of her life's work: *After Leaving Mr Mackenzie* was published in 1931, *Voyage in the Dark* in 1934 and *Good Morning Midnight* in 1939. She married her literary agent, Leslie Tilden Smith, in 1934. Two years later, the couple visited Dominica, nearly thirty years after Jean Rhys had left it. It was the only time she was ever to return to her home island.

When the Second World War broke out, Jean Rhys sank into oblivion and her books went out of print. If *Voyage in the Dark* had been reasonably successful and praised by the critics, *Good Morning Midnight* (1939) was deemed too depressing in the context of the oncoming war and received a cool welcome. She, however, never stopped writing, short stories in particular, but there is evidence that it was also about that time that she started working at the first draft of *Wide Sargasso Sea*. Leslie Tilden Smith died from a heart attack shortly after demobilization in 1945. Jean Rhys married his cousin, Max Hamer, in 1947, and they moved to a house in Beckenham. There, it appears that Jean Rhys had a rather stormy relationship with her neighbours, which brought her to court a number of times and even to the hospital of Holloway Prison. Found guilty of assault, she was bound over for a year and then put on probation for two years. To cap it all, Max Hamer was also arrested in 1950 for financial fraud. He was sentenced to three years' imprisonment and sent to Maidstone Prison. When he was released, the couple eventually managed to leave Beckenham and moved to Bude, Cornwall.

In the middle of all these difficulties, on 5 November 1949, the *New Statesman* advertised for Jean Rhys: the advertisement had been placed by an actress, Selma Vaz Dias, who had adapted *Good Morning Midnight* into a dramatic monologue to be broadcast by the BBC; she needed Jean Rhys's permission to perform it. In fact, Selma Vaz Dias gave a public performance of her adaptation, but the BBC turned it down. Jean Rhys was being rediscovered, but it was not until 1957 that the real 'discovery' occurred, when the BBC went ahead with the broadcast of *Good Morning Midnight*. Francis Wyndham, then an editor working with the publishing firm André Deutsch, came to hear of her. He had been a long-time admirer and had thought her dead, like so many others. They met and André Deutsch bought the option on her new novel. The completion of *Wide Sargasso Sea* took nine long years, hindered as Jean Rhys was by self-doubt, illness – she had a heart attack in 1964 – age and Max's deteriorating health. Still, elated by the renewed interest people seemed to take in her books and encouraged by Francis Wyndham, who helped her sell several of her wartime stories, she worked on. Her brother bought a bungalow in Cheriton Fitzpaine, Devon, where she and Max moved in 1960. Max Hamer died in 1966 and *Wide Sargasso Sea* was finally published in the same year. It brought Jean Rhys recognition, prizes and money. Her novels were all reissued, while some of her new stories were published in a collection entitled *Tigers Are Better-Looking* (1968), which included a selection from *The Left Bank*. She was made a Fellow of the Royal Society of Literature and a CBE. Although she was already in her seventies when *Wide Sargasso Sea* was published, she continued to write: she produced a number of short stories collected in *Sleep It Off Lady*, published in 1976, and, four years before she died, she undertook to write her autobiography, *Smile Please*, which was left unfinished and was published posthumously. Jean Rhys died on 14 May 1979.

Jean Rhys is an elusive figure. A white West Indian who spent most of her wandering life in Great Britain and other European countries, she never really belonged anywhere, nor did she claim membership of any group of writers or artists, not even that of the Anglo-Saxon expatriates in Paris with whom she had rubbed shoulders in the 1920s. Although she wrote all her life, from the early 1920s to the late 1970s, she was never conspicuous on the literary scene and altogether remained out of the public eye for about twenty years, until the publication of her last novel and the much publicized circumstances of her 'discovery' hurled her into the foreground. The great variety of critical response to her work is but a reflection of her elusiveness and of the indefinable quality of her texts.

Apart from early approaches which considered her fiction as thinly disguised autobiography, academic criticism falls into three main trends. One reading of Jean Rhys is to consider her as a Caribbean writer. This is what Wally Look Lai does in the first academic study of *Wide Sargasso Sea*, published in 1968.[4] Such an identification, however, cannot go without qualification. In Kenneth Ramchand's book on Caribbean literature, Jean Rhys features in a *marginal* group of 'white West Indians' alongside Phyllis Shand Allfrey, Geoffrey Drayton and J. B. Emtage, all four writers voicing the 'terrified consciousness' of the dispossessed colonizer.[5] In 1986, Teresa O'Connor issued a full-length book, *Jean Rhys: The West Indian Novels*, in which, as the title suggests, only *Voyage in the Dark* and *Wide Sargasso Sea* are discussed.[6] For such is the main difficulty of the Caribbean approach: it fails to take into account those of Jean Rhys's texts which do not refer to her home island – *Quartet*, *After Leaving Mr Mackenzie*, *Good Morning Midnight* and a substantial number of short stories.

Another critical response has been to situate Jean
Rhys in the context of literary modernism. By 1939, the
bulk of her fiction had been published and Thomas F.
Staley, for instance, sees in modernism an apt way of
categorizing Jean Rhys's works, including *Wide Sargasso
Sea* (1966). That Jean Rhys's writing shares some of the
characteristics of modernist prose cannot be denied,
especially where the emphasis on subjectivity and the
attention paid to form are concerned. As early as 1927,
Ford Madox Ford had underlined Jean Rhys's 'singular
instinct for form' in his preface to *The Left Bank*.[7] In
turn, Thomas F. Staley refers to 'her sense of proportion
and design'[8] and goes on to list the distinctly modernist
features to be found in her work:

> central to modernist art is the concept, best exempli-
> fied in English by Joyce and Eliot, of the impersonal-
> ity of the artist [...] which entailed a conscious
> artistry, a predilection for the formal properties and
> organic elements of art, a deep commitment to the
> allusive, the mythic, and a subordination of the
> traditional narrative concerns of the realistic novel
> such as plot, event, and resolution of the characters'
> circumstances.[9]

Again, Thomas F. Staley admits, qualifications have to be
made: 'Rhys's art shares many of these characteristics
and impulses of literary modernism, but she was
unaware of or removed from many of its preoccupations.'[10] Although she started to write at a time when
modernism was in full swing, under the patronage of
Ford Madox Ford – who spared no pains to promote
the movement – and in spite of the fact that she met a
lot of the modernist expatriates through Ford, Jean
Rhys remained a marginal modernist – in much the

same way as she is a marginal Caribbean writer – and outlived the movement by quite a few decades. As Helen Carr points out,

> [i]f one wants a label, 'modernist' is certainly the most satisfactory. Yet there are some elements in her work which can be better understood in terms of her affinity with the French nineteenth-century precursors of modernism, and others which might be better described as postmodernist, not least the metafictional structure of her most famous novel, *Wide Sargasso Sea*.[11]

According to Judith Kegan Gardiner, *Good Morning Midnight* itself encapsulates Jean Rhys's departure from the preoccupations of such women modernists as Colette or Virginia Woolf. Jean Rhys, she argues, found modernist irony too disengaged for the depressing realities of the times: '[s]he does not accuse them [Colette and Woolf] of being hypocritical escapists like the rich woman who hired Sasha, but she does imply that Colette's vision of ageless female sensuality and Woolf's of independent female authorship are blurred by privileges of class and national tradition'.[12] Like Judith Kegan Gardiner, many critics have seen Jean Rhys's fiction as an exploration of the disempowerment of women at the hands of male oppressors. The discovery of Jean Rhys's works by academia coincided with the development of women's studies, a chance encounter which, due to the thematic content of the texts, developed into a steady, if sometimes strained, relationship. Most feminist critics have concerned themselves with the representation of women in Jean Rhys's fiction. The first full-length study of it delineates 'the Rhys woman' through an archetypal framework based on female myths and Freudian and

Jungian models.[13] More frequently, Jean Rhys's works
have been seen in terms of sexual power politics, which
has led some feminists, those in search of consciousness-
raising role-models, to resent the heroines' collaborative
attitude and debilitating passivity. In the late 1980s,
Rhysian critics started to pay increasing attention to the
discursive implications of the issue of femininity. Nancy
R. Harrison is a case in point. Trying to delineate the
specificity of a woman's writing, she identifies the ways
in which the feminine speaks back to the patriarchal
order in a contrapuntal idiom, in a subtext which
develops 'in the interstices of the "real" dialogue' and
will in time be made to become the dominant text in
Jean Rhys's practice.[14] Deborah Kelly Kloepfer also
explores Jean Rhys's feminist poetics but from a
different perspective: probing into the feminine economy of loss, she concentrates on the suppressed mother
languages in Jean Rhys's texts.[15]

Critics have lately tended to blend all three
approaches, gender, colonialism and modernism. The
purpose of Coral Ann Howells, for instance, is to show
that Jean Rhys constructs 'a feminine colonial sensibility
becoming aware of itself in a modernist European
context, where a sense of colonial dispossession and
displacement is focused on and translated into gendered
terms, so that all these conditions coalesce, transformed
into her particular version of feminine pain'.[16] Weaving
together three theoretical systems is probably the right
thing to do, but it is also a very challenging task which
might be carried out at the expense of close readings of
the texts. Mine is a primarily textual bias. I shall be
looking at the textual inscription of the feminine in each
of Jean Rhys's novels as well as in some of her short
fiction. Jean Rhys's poetics, it will be argued, seeks to
subvert – and not just to invert – any ideological model.
Her version of the feminine is a deconstructive force

which undermines any form of authority. Instead of examining her 'passion for stating the case of the underdog', as Ford Madox Ford once put it,[17] instead of looking for a mirror-image of women's subjection in the recurring motifs of oppression, I shall trace the manipulations of narrative and discursive forms which expose and destabilize the conventions of the symbolic order. Feminine dissent, in Jean Rhys's practice, takes the shape of resistance to narrative and semantic closure and makes the most of the subversive potential of irony, parodic mimicry and intertextuality in particular. Breaking finite limits or parodying mortiferous, authoritarian formulae, Jean Rhys seeks to coin a new idiom, a rhetoric of the feminine: '[s]ometimes I long for an entirely new way of writing. New words, new everything – sometimes I am almost there. But no – it slides away', she says in one of her letters.[18] This alternative signifying mode she achieves in her last novel, through her reworking of *Jane Eyre* and her revision of Gothic romance, which provide the ultimate dislocation of the dominant idiom.

2 *Quartet*: The 'Authored' Woman

When confronted with Jean Rhys's narratives, the reader may think of Rosalind Coward's question: 'Are women's novels feminist novels?'[1] Of course, Jean Rhys states various cases of women's oppression by patriarchal society, but her heroines' attitude towards their predicament as women is more often than not problematic. Far from seeking emancipation, they seem to apply themselves to cultivating their subjection. This collaborative tendency is particularly prominent in the first novel, *Quartet*, published in 1928, in which a young woman, Marya Zelli, left alone in Paris as her husband serves a year's sentence in prison, is manipulated by the Heidlers, the couple who 'rescue' her from loneliness and destitution. What *Quartet* is based upon is the typical scenario of a woman's victimization, which leads Coral Ann Howells, for example, to describe it as 'a Modernist version of Gothic'.[2] Moreover, inspired by Jean Rhys's affair with Ford Madox Ford, who was then living with Stella Bowen and supervised Jean Rhys's advent as a writer,[3] *Quartet* may be seen as giving Susan Gubar a case in point when she argues that twentieth-century women often see 'the emergence of their talent as an infusion from a male master' who 'causes the woman writer to feel her words are being expressed from her rather than by her'.[4] To be sure, Jean Rhys's narrative does not unsettle the traditional balance of power between the sexes. The whole novel proves to be an objectifying apparatus, thus mimicking the androcentric mode of discourse that relegates women to the position

10

of the spoken rather than that of the speaker. In accordance with this traditional relegation, Marya is lavishly spoken of and never achieves the status of a subject. Through her somewhat complacent depiction of the female plight, however, Jean Rhys subverts masculine order by showing how this objectifying undermines the dynamics of the narrative and leads to narrative paralysis.

Passivity

From the start, Marya Zelli clearly assumes a traditional gender role, that of the passive woman. This might be seen as paradoxical for, as the main protagonist, she is supposed to be the main prop of action in the novel. Functionally speaking, the dynamics of plot greatly depend on her. And yet, Marya is a supremely static heroine, which legitimizes the novel's alternative title, *Postures*.[5] Motionless and idle is how she is first seen in the opening lines. She kills time in a Montparnasse café and wanders around the Left Bank for no particular reason. Marya's habitual occupation is to do nothing, as she herself says to Miss de Solla, an acquaintance of hers, whom she meets by chance (Q, 7). The plot proper actually starts thanks to this subsidiary character, who asks Marya to her studio, thus creating purpose for Marya's wanderings. A chance encounter, not the heroine's initiative, is what originates the story.

The next episode, set in Miss de Solla's studio, provides a confirmation of Marya's status as an essentially passive being and therefore a functionally defective heroine. To Miss de Solla, who casts a painter's eye on the young woman, Marya is 'a decorative little person' (Q, 8). She can indeed be considered as 'decorative' in the sense that she never seems to get involved, never makes decisions and always submits to the desires of others. Instead of deciding to stay with the Heidlers, she is persuaded to move to their home against her will. She responds to invitations throughout the novel, making a guest of herself, in other people's houses as well as in her own life. Only once does she become a hostess and even then the role is forced upon her by the Heidlers, who send an envoy to check up on her. Asking Miss Nicholson to lunch turns into a distressing experience of entrapment, metaphorically represented by the setting, a zoo, and by a young fox pitifully running up and down its cage (Q, 124).

As a rule, then, Marya 'bows the head and submits', especially to the mouthpieces of patriarchal order, whether male or female. Her landlady, Madame Hautchamp, is one of them: 'Madame Hautchamp was formidable. One heard the wheels of society clanking as she spoke' (Q, 31). With her less 'formidable' husband whom she deems remarkably 'inconsistent', Marya proves to be equally obedient when he demands that she put an end to her aimless long walks. She simply complies and spends hours in her bedroom at the Hôtel de l'Univers, reading books (Q, 10). Stephan's objection to her wanderings has far-reaching consequences: it denies Marya the field of action, of direct confrontation with the world, and reduces her space to the size of a cell. This denial is ironically signalled by the name of the hotel. Instead of exploring the world, Marya has to stay within the confines of a diminutive version of it. Moreover, instead of making her own discoveries and of investing the world with the self's own fabrication of meaning, Marya has to turn to prefabricated meaning, to a world encoded by books. By being denied the field of action, she is also denied the position of the subject in the construction of meaning.

The Woman as Object

Subjected to the desires of others and deprived of the means through which she could become the conductor of action, Marya's functional justification as the heroine of *Quartet* is that she is the main object of discourse. First of all, of narratorial discourse: *Quartet* is a third-person narrative, in which Marya is by definition spoken of. Even in the passages where she is granted relative expressive autonomy, the feeling prevails that she is a defective speaker. Section 16 is a good example of her difficulty in handling speech. Most of the section reproduces Marya's indirect internal monologue, narrative discourse receding before the voice of the heroine. Yet, instead of establishing Marya as the perceiving consciousness and the origin of speech, section 16 brings her silencing to the fore:

> She never reacted now. She was a thing. Quite dead. Not a kick left in her. (*Q*, 96)

A voiceless thing just when she is indirectly given a voice, Marya can only tell us how submissive and silent she is. Even when she dreams of violent rebellion against this forced subjection, she does not really dream of speaking back but of putting a stop to Lois's objectifying logorrhoea by smashing a wine bottle in her face (*Q*, 97).

Scenes in which Marya is spoken of, including in her presence, are legion. As early as her first encounter with the Heidlers, Marya is objectified into a 'she', a grammatical anomaly – given the enunciative context – upon which the text duly comments:

> They discussed eating, cooking, England and, finally, Marya, whom they spoke of in the third person as if she were a strange animal or at any rate a strayed animal – one not quite of the fold. (*Q*, 12)

Here, Marya is a mere heading. Through the use of the third-person pronoun, she is re-created as an object one can appropriate and dispose of. A few pages later, she indeed appears as the couple's property when Lois suggests that they all go to the funfair at Luna-park to watch Marya 'being banged a bit' on the joy wheel, just for the fun of it for, after all, Marya 'ought to sing for her supper' (Q, 67). The price of Marya's supper is not just a song. Her objectifying is completed when Marya comes to the realization that her own discourse apes that of the Heidlers. Dispossessed of her own voice as a subject, she is not only an object of discourse but she seems to be possessed, duplicating a text which other people have 'authored':

> It seemed to her that, staring at the couple, she had hypnotized herself into thinking, as they did, that her mind was part of their minds. (Q, 76)

The phrasing suggests that Marya herself creates the conditions of her own victimization. She collaborates with the agents of her reification.

Closing Meaning

The form as well as the content of the story collude in carrying out Marya's entrapment. If the Heidlers determine Marya's role as an object, the narrative perfects this objectifying by closing meaning, thus imitating masculine, prescriptive discourse. Of Jean Rhys's narratives, *Quartet* is the most 'talkative' one in the sense that it carefully channels the reader's interpretation by glossing the content of the story it tells us. If, generally speaking, Jean Rhys is fond of indirect modes of signification, ambiguity or indeterminacy,

Quartet spells things out, sometimes to the point of informative redundancy.

An aspect of this tendency to closure is the frequent presence of interpretative passages that frame key scenes and guide the reader into an unequivocal reading of the scene. In Brunoy, for example, a place just outside Paris where the trio spends a tense week-end (section 14), Marya's long-suppressed violence breaks out for all-too obvious reasons. At the end of the episode, the narrative provides a synthetic summary of the scene:

> [Marya] had felt like a marionette, as though something outside her were jerking strings that forced her to scream and strike. (*Q*, 82)

Driving the point home, the narrative indicates how it should be read, and this redundant piece of information reinforces Marya's objectifying, thanks to the commonplace metaphor of the puppet.

On many occasions, the narrative also introduces doublings which greatly contribute to semantic closure and narrative redundancy. The heroine's reification is duplicated at different levels. Thus Marya, an automaton in the clutches of the Heidlers' will, is moreover represented as an object of representation. Logically enough, given the setting of the story, the cosmopolitan Left Bank of the 1920s, *Quartet* numbers many artists among its characters: Miss de Solla is a painter; Cairn writes short stories; Lois, herself an amateur painter, knows quite a few fashionable writers; Heidler's job is to discover young talent and Stephan is – officially at least – a 'commissionnaire d'objets d'art' (*Q*, 16). Among this crowd of creators, Marya stands as a creation of others, like Pygmalion's ivory girl. Sitting for Lois, for example, Marya is subjected to Lois's vision of her, a vision that tends to annihilate the modelling individual as suggested by the artist's foregrounding of dress: 'Lois had decided that she wished to begin her portrait of the sleeveless dress and the short black gloves at once' (Q, 47). She does not even paint Marya so much as a particular outfit. The model's passivity and reification are once more brought to the fore. Motionless, staring blankly, Marya is moreover the silent narratee of stories told by Lois. Again, Marya does not construct meaning; she is the sign, the text or the canvas while others hold the pen or the brush. Here Jean Rhys only mildly revises a long tradition identifying the author as a male and the female as his passive creation. As it happens, in this case the author or the painter is a woman, but she is nonetheless a representative of patriarchy. As Marya notes somewhere else, Lois is the 'species wife' (Q, 76), living out one of the few scripts androcentrism prescribes for women. As always in Jean Rhys's fiction, gender roles overlap the traditional boundaries between biological categories.

Part of the narrative's strategy to close meaning is the introduction of doubles of Marya. The most significant one is the Spanish singer who performs in a Parisian cabaret and whose number is the object of a careful evaluation by the trio. The whole episode (Q, 68–9) is a kind of *mise en abyme* of the novel, thus partaking of the metanarrative with which the novel has equipped its story. The young singer is obviously another version of Marya. Like Marya in previous years, she is on the stage; both of them are frail creatures, childlike women, the type Lois feels responsible for. Their likeness is also underlined by the fact that Lois's adverse comments on the weak-looking performer are clearly directed at Marya. She generally disapproves of weakness, we are told, be it in the singer who unconvincingly stabs her lover 'with a little feeble gesture and a sweet and simple smile' (*Q*, 69) or, implicitly, in Marya. Through her gloss of the performance and in accordance with her taste for classification and her normative nature, Lois delineates the generic category to which both young women belong: tragedy downgraded into cheap melodrama. The singer as well as Marya fail to reach tragic grandeur, it seems, because of their inability to act – in both senses of the word. Unable to turn intentions into action, they get stuck within the melodramatic posture of the victimized weakling and remain subjected to their fate, here embodied by the Heidlers, a parodic version of tragic *fatum*. The episode can be seen as the enactment of a masculine encoding of a woman, revealing how certain options are denied to women while others are assigned to them. It also lends an insight into how the narrative constructs meaning. The doublings and mirror-effects build up semantic walls around the heroine. Redundancy of information is another possible incarnation of fate at the level of the structure of the narrative.

For the tyranny of fate is in fact no other than the tyranny of the signified. The principal agent of closure or semantic limitation is Lois's commentary, which is part of the self-interpretative system that accompanies the story. Lois is one of the main supports of this system and her normative approach reflects the way in which *Quartet* delineates its signified. Lois's function is to impersonate a particular discursive practice, within which Marya is trapped. She has no alternative except to conform to the pre-written scripts available to her. In Coral Ann Howells's words, Marya is 'a blank space allowing herself to be constructed through other people's narratives'.[6] In this way, she starts as the inexperienced girl, slave to the romantic fantasy of falling in love with Heidler; then she is cast into the stereotype of the prostitute by other mouthpieces of masculine discourse. One of them is Monsieur Lefranc, the proprietor of a restaurant the trio

often goes to. He is one of the voices of public opinion in
Quartet and as such, Monsieur Lefranc reads Marya as a
'*grue*' when he detects at first sight that she and Heidler
are having an affair (*Q*, 66). His task is not so much to
decipher a fairly obvious situation as to read it along the
lines of the text of culture, thus turning Marya into
a recognizable, predictable figure one can give a name to.
Again, the narrative reproduces an ideological encoding
of the heroine. Her semantic label is a preconstructed
given, a closed entity, which implies that no real development is possible. This is what the narrative suggests
as it shortly afterwards represents Marya as one of
those *grues*, surrendering to the stereotype or even
reconstructing it.

Just as Marya at last tries to break away from the
Heidlers with high hopes of finding an identity of her
own, she in fact conforms even more adequately to the
script Monsieur Lefranc has so eloquently 'written'.
Moving into the Hôtel du Bosphore (section 15), with its
'atmosphere of departed and ephemeral loves' and
vaguely erotic furnishings (*Q*, 87), she also moves even
closer to the status of the *grue*. In this all but virtuous
environment, Marya is now one item in a long line of
predecessors and, like them before her, she is invested
with a particular function defined by pre-existing codes,
implying a particular outfit and 'savoir faire':

> It was impossible, when one looked at that bed, not to
> think of the succession of *petites femmes* who had
> extended themselves upon it, clad in carefully
> thought out pink or mauve chemises, full of tact,
> and savoir faire and savoir vivre and all the rest of it.
> (*Q*, 87)

The phrase designating Marya's new function, '*petites
femmes*', reads as a stylistic analogon to her entrapment.

A stock phrase ossified by repetitive usage, it mimics her reification. The repetitive script which she is being forced into is moreover replicated in the endless line of trains in the Montparnasse station nearby, 'where all day a succession of shabby trains, each trailing its long scarf of smoke, clanked slowly backwards and forwards' (*Q*, 87). These trains seem far removed from any idea of escapism: paradoxically weighed down with smoke, weary, they come and go instead of departing. Marya herself is part of all these abortive departures, caught as she is in the flow of repetitions and of male paradigms for female experience.

Narrative Paralysis

Once Marya conforms to the stereotype which masculine discourse has imposed upon her, the narrative seems to get stuck, experiencing an entrapment that bears a certain likeness to that of Marya. Having led its protagonist to conformity to traditional gender roles with no possibility of an escape, *Quartet* condemns itself to mere repetition of a pre-written text. The narrative seems to be affected by paralysis, both from the point of view of its imagery and of its dynamics, especially from the middle of the novel (section 12) onwards. Section 12 comes after the episode in which Marya finally responds to Heidler's advances, thus becoming the couple's thing. Marya's disappearance as a subject then materializes in proliferating images of hypnotic motionlessness and confinement:

> She felt hypnotized as she listened to him [Heidler], impotent. (*Q*, 70)

> she was caught in this appalling muddle. (*Q*, 70)

she was in a frenzy of senseless fright. Fright of a child
shut up in a dark room. Fright of an animal caught in
a trap. (Q, 71)

The trap closes in upon Marya and her gradual sinking
into a vegetative state is evinced by the development of
the isotopy of the prison that runs throughout the novel.
Imprisonment is the organizing principle of *Quartet*: the
story starts a few days before Stephan's arrest, the direct
cause of Marya's misfortune, and ends a few days after his
liberation. A parallel is to be drawn between the two
characters. There lies the function of Stephan in the
narrative: if he is the fourth component announced by
the title, he is much more so as a metaphor of Marya's
entrapment than as the betrayed husband. Five of
Marya's visits to the parlour of the prison are staged in
the course of the story, each visit building up a gradual
converging of the two characters' experiences. At first,
Marya feels utterly estranged from the prison and its
inmates. In the deafening din of the parlour, for
example, it is as if a dumb-show were taking place.
Marya who, all of a sudden, seems to be unable to
understand French, can no longer make sense of what
her gesticulating husband is saying to her (Q, 31). Little
by little, however, although Marya and Stephan gradually become strangers, Marya experiences a growing
feeling of familiarity with those she calls the 'under-dog'
(Q, 85), a feeling that soon develops into effusive passion:

Soon, [...] she extended this passion to all the
inmates of the prison, to the women who waited with
her under the eye of the fat warder, to all unsuccess-
ful and humbled prostitutes, to everybody who wasn't
plump, sleek, satisfied, smiling and hard-eyed. [...]
To everybody, in fact, who was utterly unlike the
Heidlers. (Q, 98)

An epiphany has taken place: Marya recognizes her own locus as one of confinement and constraint. But one has to draw a line between Stephan's imprisonment and hers, for Stephan is soon to be liberated, while Marya's emancipation is not on the agenda. On the contrary, the narrative, as it unfolds, shows a marked tendency towards restricting the heroine's options.

Marya's passivity, for example, evolves into sheer indifference in the last third of the novel. Up to then, she is decidedly passive but still driven by desire, and she sometimes manages to articulate her resistant view by criticizing Lois or rebelling against the oppression of the couple. As the narrative draws to an end, however, Marya's attempts at intervention in patriarchal discourse disappear. Apathy and indifference overcome, as manifested by the way in which a chance encounter with another lover is represented. Towards the end of the narrative, a young man approaches Marya and asks her to his flat: ' "[w]hy not?" said Marya. "What's it matter?" ' (*Q*, 118). Automatic compliance is a sign of Marya's increasing detachment. What the young man says to keep the conversation going is transcribed in indirect discourse as if Marya was a passive receptacle of his words rather than an active interlocutor. At this stage she lacks substance so much that she cannot even sustain a real dialogue. The text reports nothing of what happens at the anonymous young man's flat. Textual elision reflects Marya's blankness.

Her new indifference is prominent in section 21 in which Marya, now rejected by the Heidlers, lies almost lifeless on a beach on the French riviera:

> The beach was strewn with old sardine tins and fishing nets spread to dry in the sun. A little white boat, called *Je m'en fous*, heaved very slowly up and down at the end of its rope. Beyond the pebbles

and the sardine tins the sea was the colour of a field
of blue hyacinths.
    Marya lay in the sun hour after hour and her
thoughts were vague and pale, like ghosts. (*Q*, 120)

Like the sardine tins, Marya has been used and disposed
of. The boat, which alone seems to breathe, is congruent
with her frame of mind and position. A discarded object,
Marya is still tethered to patriarchal order but no longer
reacts, even silently. Her mind has gone blank. Her
objectifying reaches a climax in abjection, a state in
which Marya is no longer a subject or an object but an
amorphous entity. This newly acquired state of abjection
is not so much a new development in Marya's life as
an extension of her previous condition. It also points to
the fact that the narrative is merely re-enacting the
degraded status of women in patriarchal ideology. Being
forbidden any alternative script, Marya in turn can only
consciously re-enact the script of humiliation and pain
that has been forced upon her, forever repeating her
abdication as a subject. This re-enactment is typical of
her relationship with Heidler: '[s]he was quivering and
abject in his arms, like some unfortunate dog abashing
itself before its master' (*Q*, 102).
    Stephan's return does not change anything in
Marya's spectral life and abjection. Instead of creating
new possibilities for her, their brief reunion confirms
Marya's entrapment. This is conveyed by her perception
of time:

    Those were strange days, detached from everything
    that had gone before or would follow after. (*Q*, 110)

Marya is now chained to the instant, with no past or
future to give her a sense of direction. Apparently fulfilled, she is nonetheless deprived of an essential element

as far as development is concerned, a future. Elsewhere, the magic spell of the instant, the temporality of ful- filment, turns into a dysphoric feeling of loss and indirection:

> A horrible nostalgia, an ache for the past seized her.
> > *Nous n'irons plus au bois;*
> > *Les lauriers sont coupés . . .*
>
> Gone, and she was caught in this appalling muddle. Life was like that. Here you are, it said, and then immediately afterwards. Where are you? (*Q*, 70–1)

In marked contrast to such perception, Heidler con- stantly projects himself into the future: utterances like '[w]e'll talk about it tomorrow' (*Q*, 70) or 'I shan't remember a thing about all this tomorrow morning' (*Q*, 82) are quite common in him. They are not mere evasions; they rather establish him as the puppet-master of Marya's future. Deprived of a dynamic temporality of her own, locked within the discrete instant, she is bound to stay within the no (wo)man's land of abjection.

Oriented duration is therefore replaced by repetition, a clue to the narrative's own incapacity to advance. As a testimony to the impossible progress of the narrative, the last section is riddled with repetitions. It is made up of two separate scenes: in the first one, Marya is sitting in a café, staring at a newspaper stand. She assumes more or less the same posture as in the opening lines, which tends to check any inclination we may have to see the plot of *Quartet* as a series of transformations. This repetition also suggests that, were the narrative to continue, it would only do so by repeating itself. The conversation that takes place between Marya and Monsieur Bernadet, a friend of Stephan's, reinforces this sense of sameness, as Monsieur Bernadet supports the idea that everything is the same in every country, an

opinion Marya can only be in full agreement with:
' "[o]ne pretends that one will find something different.
It's only a game" ' (Q, 135). After Bernadet's departure,
Marya undertakes to re-read a letter from Heidler,
another form of repetition. The letter says he wishes to
see her. Things have now become so predictable that
Marya mentally reconstructs the meeting:

> When and where? In some café, of course. The
> unvarying background. Knowing waiters, clouds of
> smoke, the smell of drink. She would sit there
> trembling, and he would be cool, a little impatient,
> perhaps a little nervous. Then she would try to
> explain and he would listen with a calm expression.
> Top dog. (Q, 137)

The proceedings and outcome are so certain that the
narrative does not even bother to actualize them.

In the second scene of section 23, Marya and Stephan
are brought together again. It is mainly a confession
scene in which Marya tells Stephan about her affair with
Heidler, thus summarizing the contents of *Quartet* in a
final doubling. Her embedded narrative merely repeats
the story, if in a simplified way. Introducing no new
element, no transformation, it can be seen as a final
manifestation of informative redundancy in the novel.
Moreover, within this iterative confession, many internal
repetitions are to be found. Marya obsessively quotes
one of Lois's utterances: ' "[w]hat's the matter with you is
that you're too virtuous" ' (Q, 139) appears four times, as
a reminder that Marya still fails to articulate a tale of
her own. Finally, Marya seems to have been prompted
into this confession against her will: ' "[i]t wasn't that
that I wanted to tell you. Because really, you see, it
doesn't matter" ' (Q, 141). Although she speaks in her
own voice – the confession is carried out in direct

speech – Marya is spoken into a text that she does not originate, just as she has been throughout the novel. The last glimpse we get of the heroine partakes of the portrayal of entrapment: she lies still after being violently jostled and thrown to the floor by Stephan. Although we do not know whether she dies or not, she is granted the posture of death, of an inanimate object, while Stephan leaves Paris. His flight, however, evokes a situation of potentially infinite repetition: Mademoiselle Chardin, who leaves with him, symptomatically bears the name of a painter of still lifes and is, in Stephan's own words, *'encore une grue'* (*Q*, 144). Narrative closure prevails, as the most effective signifier of entrapment.

Through the destiny of Marya, which is not unique as the appearance of this Mademoiselle Chardin suggests, Jean Rhys represents the predetermined gender roles patriarchal order writes upon women. Does Jean Rhys's intervention in androcentric discourse merely consist in the exposure of traditional power games? Her work has little to gain from a purely semantic approach for, where theme is concerned, she offers no significant break-through in terms of feminist dissent. Certainly, *Quartet* carefully delineates conventional identifications of women as objects and even examines women's own contribution to their entrapment in the shape of romantic fantasies of falling in love and of self-abandonment to male mastery. However, Jean Rhys's resistant voice is more likely to be heard in her handling of narrative form rather than content. As far as *Quartet* is concerned, Jean Rhys's dissident statement lies in her mastery of narrative redundancy and closure as a formal duplication of the paralysis women are subjected to. Marya being, as she demonstrates, a pre-constructed given, a stereotypical text, Jean Rhys establishes her novel as mere repetition of consensus, deliberately leading it to narrative deadlock. This is where the subversive dimension of the novel lies. The feminine, then, should be traced in the metatext rather than the subtext of Marya's silent and useless rebellions.

3 *After Leaving Mr Mackenzie*: 'Between Dog and Wolf'

In *After Leaving Mr Mackenzie*, her second novel published in 1930, Jean Rhys approaches the problem of feminine identity in a radically different way. In marked contrast to Marya Zelli, Julia Martin, a middle-aged woman, will not 'allow herself to be constructed through other people's narratives'. An elusive figure cast adrift in Paris and London after the break-up of her relationship with the eponymous character, she baffles those who come across her and defeats any attempt they might make to define her. An exile in every possible way, she is cut off from her relatives, lives outside her country as a social outcast, and cannot be incorporated into known categories. A borderline character, 'between dog and wolf', to borrow the novel's last words, she is destined for marginal existence and indeterminacy. In fact, in her first two novels, Jean Rhys seems to be playing with the trope of the blank page. She exploits it in two distinct ways, as female authors often do, according to Susan Gubar. In *Quartet*, Jean Rhys uses the metaphor 'to expose how woman has been defined symbolically in the patriarchy as a tabula rasa, a lack, a negation, an absence'.[1] Marya is a blank page in the sense that she is passively written upon, 'authored' by those who hold the pen. In *After Leaving Mr Mackenzie*, Jean Rhys turns the

trope into an instrument of dissent and a defiant
statement. If Julia Martin is a blank page, it is because
she will not be written upon. Blankness then opens up a
world of infinite possibility, as opposed to the limited
options available to women in masculine discourse. *After
Leaving Mr Mackenzie* elaborates another conception
of blankness as a potent act of resistance meant to
circumvent semantic entrapment. The dynamics of the
narrative are revitalized in the process.

The Missing Face

The narrative strategy of *After Leaving Mr Mackenzie* in
terms of characterization is obliquely announced at the
beginning of the novel in the shape of an ironic
comment on the work of a celebrated sculptor who, we
are told, 'reduces everybody's ego to an egg' (*ALM*, 29).
Far from constructing this egg-shaped ego, *After Leaving
Mr Mackenzie* shatters the boundaries of the self and
pulverizes it into scattered fragments, making it difficult
for the reader to operate the reduction the sculptor – as
well as *Quartet* to a certain extent – successfully achieves.

This strategy is exemplified by the way in which the
narrating voice draws the portrait of Julia Martin, the
heroine. In *Quartet*, the portrayal of the protagonist is
taken up by a knowing, intrusive narrator who does not
seek to conceal his/her omniscience:

> Marya, you must understand, had not been suddenly
> and ruthlessly transplanted from solid comfort to the
> hazards of Montmartre. Nothing like that. Truth to
> say, she was used to a lack of solidity and of fixed
> backgrounds. (*Q*, 14)

In *After Leaving Mr Mackenzie*, however, omniscience
does not seem to apply. The heterodiegetic narrator[2]

seems to be reluctant to carry out one of his/her traditional tasks, that is, introducing the cast of characters through physical description and biographical summary. The description of Julia's physical appearance is delayed by the depiction of her hotel room, for example: furniture, decoration and personal belongings are granted exhaustive descriptions, focused through Julia's point of view – the narrator steps back – while looking-glasses, which generally introduce portraits in traditional novel-writing, go missing or consistently deny the reader the heroine's reflection:

> There was a wardrobe without a looking-glass, a red plush sofa and – opposite the bed and reflecting it – a very spotted mirror in a gilt frame. (*ALM*, 8)

It is not until page 10 that Julia's features eventually take shape, although in a rather sketchy way. The spare information the reader is reluctantly given about Julia's looks is then immediately followed by a passage in which the narrator claims he/she cannot be much more specific about Julia:

> Her career of ups and downs had rubbed most of the hall-marks off her, so that it was not easy to guess at her age, her nationality, or the social background to which she properly belonged. (*ALM*, 11)

In this sentence, the narrator officially gives up omniscience, conferring on the reader the task of gathering the relevant information in the course of the narrative. Clues to Julia's age, nationality, past, and so on, are strewn all over the text, sparingly palliating the incompleteness of the portrait in a discontinuous way. The reader is left to fill in the blanks while the ostentatiously imperfect knowledge of the narrating voice posits Julia as an incomplete, indeterminate character.

The narrator's fake puzzlement when it comes to describing Julia is duplicated in subsidiary characters such as the owner of the Hôtel Saint Raphaël where Julia is staying. First the landlady is suspicious and inquisitive, then, mystified by Julia's strange existence, she just has to 'cease to speculate' (*ALM*, 9). The distinctive feature of this heroine, who otherwise has 'no visible scars', is that she triggers off hermeneutic activity and makes positive 'labelling' impossible. Horsfield, her new lover, comes up against the same opacity. Like a 'private eye', he investigates, observes, infers, yet never comes to any conclusion. Like everybody else, he finds it hard to 'read' this woman and time will be no help: he will never solve the riddle. At some stage, he complains that 'one can never know what the woman is really feeling' (*ALM*, 111) and her face is so immune to portrayal that he hardly remembers what she looks like (*ALM*, 56).

The text's deliberate vagueness about Julia is all the more striking as the narrating voice occasionally shows its capacity to be much more definite about other characters such as Norah, Julia's sister, who lives in London and takes care of their invalid mother. Norah, it seems, is extremely decodable and the narrator is willing to do the decoding: 'Norah herself was labelled for all to see. She was labelled "Middle class, no money"' (*ALM*, 53). The same assertive tone prevails in the description of Mr Mackenzie, although he is a more complex character. First the narrator shows his/her competence by delineating the type into which Mr Mackenzie can be incorporated:

> Mr Mackenzie was a man of medium height and colouring. He was of the type which proprietors of restaurants and waiters respect. He had enough nose to look important, enough stomach to look benevolent. (*ALM*, 17)

The facts about the character are then stated directly: he is forty-eight, made a lot of money in early life, retired and now lives on a comfortable income (*ALM*, 18). In the case of Mr Mackenzie, the narrator is also able to detect the contradictions and weaknesses lurking beneath the mask of respectability. In spite of Mackenzie's remarkable adaptation to the social system, 'some kink in his nature – that volume of youthful poems perhaps still influencing him – [...] morbidly attracted him to strangeness, to recklessness, even unhappiness' (*ALM*, 18–19). This substantially detailed portrait makes it clear that, as the occasion arises, the narrator is perfectly capable of decoding the decodable. In the case of Julia, however, decoding is problematic: cultural grids fail to categorize her and the narrator chooses not to violate her blankness. As opposed to Mr Mackenzie and his lawyer, both 'perfectly represent[ing] organized society' (*ALM*, 17), Julia is an outlaw evading the law of the father and challenging the power of naming.

The most significant emblem of her 'lawlessness' is the metaphoric mask she wears throughout the novel. Make-up plays a prominent role in her life. In her hotel room, the only signs of Julia's presence consist of a whole range of cosmetics (*ALM*, 8). In place of Julia's reflection in the mirror, the text lists the ingredients with which she elaborates her mask, which, we are told, has 'long ceased to be a labour of love' (*ALM*, 11). Time and again in the story, she powders her face in a mechanical way. This 'inevitable, absent-minded gesture' (*ALM*, 65) can be related to the blank page as a trope for female creativity. According to Susan Gubar, the woman's interest in cosmetics or fashion is induced by her exclusion from active artistic creation. Unable to become artists for historical reasons, women tended to work in private, using the only materials at hand, their bodies and selves, thus turning themselves into artistic

objects. This 'ornamental behaviour', as Susan Gubar
calls it, provides women with their only chance of getting
to shape things. Julia's painting her face is then typical of
'the deflection of female creativity from the production
of art to the recreation of the body'.[3] Make-up and
clothing are not designed to conceal the true self; they
actually create identity while defeating 'legal' taxonomy. In the case of Mr Mackenzie, the true self is to be
found beneath his posturing as a respectable gentleman.
The mask of respectability serves to hide a potentially
destructive vulnerability. The task of the narrator is then
to unmask the character. As far as Julia is concerned, no
unmasking will be undertaken, for nothing lies beneath
the make-up – her face is hardly described. Julia is a
virgin page on which she writes her own text. The mask
thus becomes a metaphor for female authorship. It also
indicates that the narrative will not follow a hermeneutic
path towards revelation and will not compete with Julia's
self-produced text. The narrator remains non-committal
or non-intrusive, not meeting the demand for certainties. The function of the heroine's mask is to make
certainties untenable and to defeat semantic closure.

Biography Versus Gynography

The disowning of controlled portrayal partakes of a
general movement towards the dismantling of prescriptive discourse in an attempt to turn female identity into an
open construct. In order to circumvent closure, the
narrative similarly disrupts the linear structure of biography and unsettles 'his-story', simultaneously laying the
ground for the birth of 'herstory'.

   Discontinuity is the (dis)organizational principle of
the representation of Julia's life and past. In spite of the

strictly chronological, integrated structure of the narrative, information is released in a disjointed manner. It is up to the reader to re-create the continuum of Julia's life. One of the main sources of information is Julia herself who, through internal monologue or dialogue, sometimes discloses a few facts about herself in such a disconnected way that she makes it difficult for the reader to reconstruct her biography. As a rule, she is reluctant to name things and places, to explain herself, as in this dialogue with Horsfield:

'Well, I told you. I left London after the armistice. What year was that?'

'Nineteen-eighteen'.

'Yes. I left in February the year after. Then I wandered about a good deal with – with the man I left London with. Most places, but not Spain or Italy. And then I came along to Paris'. (*ALM*, 37)

In this particular instance, naming Spain or Italy as places where she did not go is an excuse for not naming the various places she actually went to. The phrase 'the man' is a deliberate evasion of the man's identity, as suggested by the dash, which betrays self-censorship. Although the facts of Julia's biography gradually become more precise, for 'the man' will eventually be identified as Julia's husband by Uncle Griffiths (*ALM*, 59), the syntagmatic distance between the two pieces of information results in a shattered signified and the reader has to put in quite a lot of work to complete the picture.

The same kinds of mental calculations on the part of the reader are necessary to situate the narrative in time. The novel maintains a paradox between the abundance of dates and time-markers and the sustained impression of discontinuity. In fact, precise dates in part generate this discontinuity. Such is the case when Julia discovers what we assume to be the menu from her wedding reception, which tells us when and where Julia got married – '*Wien, le 24 août, 1920*' (*ALM*, 30) – and reminds her of what she wore on her wedding day. The narrative then abruptly returns to its main line, making such precise indications seem gratuitous, as they do not introduce any explanatory flashback that might significantly contribute to the completion of the picture. Precise dating is then merely indicative of a lack of elaboration, of the fragmentation or indeterminacy of the representation of Julia's past. Instead of anchoring her biography in history, dates paradoxically signal the deconstruction of linear biography, enhancing the missing connections in Julia's remembrances.

Such deconstruction suggests that *After Leaving Mr Mackenzie* may primarily concern itself with the anxieties of representation and the ways and means of storytelling from a female perspective. It is most apparent in an episode in which Horsfield and Julia are breaking the ice (*ALM*, 37–43). Explaining that it is not always easy or beneficial to talk about oneself, Julia tells him how she once tried to tell the story of her life to a woman sculptor she used to sit for. Far from providing occasion for a full-length account of her past life, her embedded narrative is responsible for a complex destabilization of identity, while passing a metafictional comment on the bafflement of representation that *After Leaving Mr Mackenzie* carries out. From the start, the narratee of Julia's story, Horsfield, seems to have difficulty in following Julia's tale. A surrogate for the reader, Horsfield accordingly interrupts her narrative and asks for clarification (*ALM*, 38). It seems that Horsfield is endowed with the task of reintroducing the missing connections in Julia's disconnected biography. However, Horsfield's questions themselves, prompted by the opacity of Julia's narrative, are interruptions which postpone the moment of revelation several times, thus adding to the narrative's discontinuity. Each of Horsfield's intrusions initiates a loop in Julia's story: a time-shift to happy days in Ostend or a psychological portrait of the sculptor (*ALM*, 39). When Julia finally takes up her story again, the reader may think that now is the time for her full-length biography: '[a]nd so one day, when we were sitting smoking, and having tea, I started to tell all about myself' (*ALM*, 39). Yet, none of this 'all about myself' will ever be conveyed to us, for Julia then operates a shift of perspective, occulting the contents of her life story to focus on the sculptor's response to it. Not only does reception act as a screen obliterating production, but the shift of perspective also blurs the boundaries between 'fiction' and 'reality', which comes as another complication on the path to revelation – Horsfield does not quite buy Julia's story (*ALM*, 38–9) and Ruth just does not believe Julia:

> 'I wanted her to understand. I felt that it was awfully important that some human being should know what I had done and why I had done it. I told everything. I went on and on.
>
> And when I had finished I looked at her. She said: "You seem to have had a hectic time". But I knew when she spoke that she didn't believe a word'. (*ALM*, 40)

What makes Julia's account unconvincing is its exhaustive quality. The restoration of causal links, in the image of correct, chronological biography, entails the collapse of meaning and identity. Julia's 'hectic' story simply does not make sense and Julia herself ends up not believing what she has just related (*ALM*, 41). Deleting Julia's life story, *After Leaving Mr Mackenzie* self-reflexively disowns the biographical model as something that cancels the

advent of the truth and makes identity falter. The
collapse of identity is metaphorized by a painting by
Modigliani, the description of which screens Julia's
unspoken biography (*ALM*, 40). The character on the
canvas, by definition without depth, wearing a mask,
bears a parodic resemblance to Julia who has failed to
reconstruct the various strata of her life. The canvas,
that '*mort plate*' as Roland Barthes calls it,[4] is a trope for
Julia's failed archaeology. However, for all its blank
posturing, the figure on the canvas appears to be more
real than Julia:

> I felt as if the woman in the picture were laughing at
> me and saying: 'I am more real than you. But at the
> same time I *am* you. I'm all that matters of you'.
>   And I felt as if all my life and all myself were
> floating away from me like smoke and there was
> nothing to lay hold of – nothing. (*ALM*, 41)

Having tried to assert her identity along the lines of
conventional biography, Julia is left with nothing. Her
attempt at 'realization' thanks to 'his-story' simply turns
her into a self-estranged spectre. This disquieting
'derealization' comes to a head when, once home, she
discovers that all her photographs, her passport,
marriage-book, and so on, have vanished: '[a]nd I was
there, like a ghost' (*ALM*, 41).

Although we do not learn much about Julia's life
story, a text is being written here. Refuting 'his-story'
(conventional biography), Julia manages to tell 'herstory' all the same. For the integrated self she seeks to
delineate in her doubly embedded narrative (the story
whose narratee is Ruth), she substitutes the representation of a proliferating subject. She features as a double
narrator operating at two different levels and skilfully
framing both narratives. She also splits into several

objects screening each other: she is the object of her unspoken biography; she models for a sculptor and identifies with the woman on the canvas. The addition of all these fragments does not result in a sum total. None of the completed objects is ever depicted, whether it be the biographical self or the statue. Closure cannot catch up with Julia's elusive identity; no synthesis is ever achieved. The section following this episode, 'The First Unknown', coincides with the end of Part One, at which point Julia is about to leave Paris. She is still on the move and remains a relative blank, outgrowing the conventional procedures of identification: '[a]fter all, I'm *not finished*. It's all nonsense that I am. I'm *not finished* at all', says Julia just before her departure (*ALM*, 45; my emphasis).

The Quest for Articulation

Julia's doubly embedded narrative, linear and exhaustive, originates a marrow-freezing dissolution of identity. Any finite picture of the heroine is discarded as inadequate and replaced by a mode of representation that makes certainty impossible. Yet, *After Leaving Mr Mackenzie* also expresses a desire for the kind of continuity afforded by chronology. Continuity, as opposed to fragmentation, is the object of a quest in the second part of the novel: Julia leaves for London with high hopes of reviving long-neglected family ties. By crossing the Channel, she is undeniably trying to get back in touch with her past, to connect her current, disoriented self with the previous one. One may argue that the trip to London is in fact a quest for connection, an attempt to restore broken bonds. Thus, if on the one hand continuity is a threat to female identity as it inevitably leads to semantic closure, it is felt, on the other hand, as a necessary component in the production of meaning without which the woman is left incomplete and equally spectral. Julia is stuck in a double bind: she has to choose between entrapment within stereotypical tags, which is a form of blankness, and self-inflicted nothingness, in the sense that openness and fragmentation do not really allow her to articulate a meaningful text. She then starts on a quest for meaning, implying the reintroduction of some kind of continuity. What she seeks in London is articulation, to be understood both as the act of jointing and of speaking. There she might find the links necessary to meaningfulness, the possibility of establishing new connections between signifiers and signifieds.

Past and identity are not pre-constructed givens in *After Leaving Mr Mackenzie*. They do not appear in the shape of definitions, descriptions or finite labels managed by an omniscient and intrusive narrator. They nonetheless feature as the object of a quest, as something you earn. *After Leaving Mr Mackenzie* could then be seen as a story of how a woman conquers an identity of her own. It is that conquest that the novel explores in its second part, by far the longest. Julia's trip to London is more of a journey in time than in space. She means to get back in touch with an old lover, her sister, her uncle, her mother, her childhood, and so on. Her stay is interspersed with memories of the past. She wants to reappropriate her roots, to bridge gaps, and is prepared to enter the fray to do so:

> She had lost the feeling of indifference to her fate, which in Paris had sustained her for so long. She knew herself ready to struggle and twist and turn, to be unscrupulous and cunning as are all weak creatures fighting for their lives against the strong. (*ALM*, 55)

The stakes are quite high. Winning back her connections, taking up things where she had left them, she might regain a sense of direction. However, Julia's quest is a failure. Far from being the place where Julia will knot together all the loose ends, London turns out to be the locus of separation and exclusion, as in Uncle Griffiths's sitting-room where, unlike two other boarders who sit cosily by the fire, Julia remains 'outside the sacred circle of warmth' (*ALM*, 57). Julia is doomed to stay 'outside the sacred circle', in the margin. Each time she tries to make a connection, she is rejected: here Uncle Griffiths condescends to giving her £1 so that she can buy a ticket back to Paris (*ALM*, 61); after Julia's mother's cremation, Miss Wyatt, her sister's companion, bluntly dismisses her (*ALM*, 101); Neil James, her old friend, gets rid of her with a £20 note and a clear intimation that this is the last she will hear of him (*ALM*, 124); the owner of the boarding-house in Notting Hill, Mrs Atherton, turns her out of her room (*ALM*, 123); at the end of her stay, Julia breaks up with Horsfield, who is only too happy not to have to do it himself (*ALM*, 126–7).

Of all the separations taking place in London, the death of Julia's mother is of course the most radical one. Returning home, Julia was hoping to recover the linkage that had once made her mother 'the warm centre of the world' (*ALM*, 77). But before she can even vaguely recapture a sense of pre-symbolic wholeness, her mother dies, leaving a gap beyond repair. An essential articulation has now gone – it actually went years before when Norah was born (*ALM*, 77) – definitely putting Julia 'outside the pale' (*ALM*, 69), forever barring her from meaning. During the funeral, she comes short of an epiphany, but meaning will not give itself away:

she was obsessed with the feeling that she was so close to seeing the thing that was behind all the talking and the posturing, and that the talking and the posturing were there to prevent her from seeing it. (*ALM*, 94)

With the death of Julia's mother, *After Leaving Mr Mackenzie* re-enacts the original separation and plunge into the symbolic order that may well give access to language, but not to signifying articulation from Julia's point of view.

As a consequence, the traditional form of the quest as motivated movement towards wish-fulfilment is subverted. First of all, the space in which it is carried out tends to shrink, causing movement to shrivel to near-motionlessness. From section 9 onwards, that is to say after her mother's death, the heroine's wanderings through London are on the wane. Section 10, entitled 'Notting Hill', clearly suggests that the open space of conquest has significantly dwindled: Julia now sticks to the neighbourhood of her boarding-house. Section 11 is entirely set within the confines of her room; its title, 'It Might Have Been Anywhere', indicates that space has simply ceased to signify. In section 12, Julia does not go out at all, except to have dinner and see a film with Horsfield in the evening. Sections 13 and 14 are equally set in the boarding-house, or even, as far as section 13 is concerned, in the cramped staircase of the boarding-house.

Even when space is still open enough to accommodate a dynamic quest, circular images interfere with the normally expansionist movement of conquest. The first section in Part Two, 'Return to London', is the first manifestation of the circularity that saps Julia's wrestling with meaning. *Returning* to London, she is bound to re-experience the various separations which, ten years before, had led her to leave England and to break off communication with her relatives. Attempting to bridge the gaps, she will only duplicate them. Accordingly, she consistently comes up against sameness and the confusion inherent to it, in the very space that was supposed to help her make sense. She loses control over space and is obsessed with the feeling that she is going round in circles. When Uncle Griffiths dismisses her, for example, Julia loses all sense of direction, bewildered by the similarity of the houses she walks by (*ALM*, 61). The streets in Notting Hill are 'like the streets of a grey dream – a labyrinth of streets, all exactly alike' (*ALM*, 84). The cityscape is haunted by repetition and seems to close in on Julia:

> It was the darkness that got you. It was heavy darkness, greasy and compelling. It made walls round you, and shut you in so that you felt you could not breathe. You wanted to beat at the darkness and shriek to be let out. (*ALM*, 62)

Walled in, suffocated by the thickness of the air, Julia sees her quest for meaning turn into an aimless, circular stroll around a central void, the missing articulation.

Insubstantiality

Returning to her past, Julia had tried to connect the various elements of her life into a significant whole. She is left with a disoriented present, a present that cannot really take shape. The references to the past, meant to restore some kind of continuity, contribute to empty the present of substance. If one refers to the title of the novel, it seems only natural that the past should interfere with Julia's present: 'after leaving Mr Mackenzie' establishes a close relationship with a traumatic past, logically haunting the present. The novel spans a transition period during which boundaries between past and present are bound to be crossed. Yet the diegetic level[5] is literally invaded by the extradiegetic past: as we have seen, the whole of the second part deals with it; in the first part, a section is entirely devoted to Mr Mackenzie, the embodiment of this extradiegetic past, and focused through him; the eponymous character also reappears in the closing section of the novel. The diegesis is moreover interspersed with time-shifts backwards. Nothing but the flimsiness of the actual diegesis can account for such disproportionate overlappings.

The plot in *After Leaving Mr Mackenzie* is remarkably thin. The isotopy of insubstantiality, combined with the treatment of time, tends to transform the diegesis into a virtual text. At the beginning of the novel, we are told that Julia has spent six months licking her wounds in a hotel, under cover, with the 'rumble of life outside' (*ALM*, 9). This interlude comes to an end with a disruption in the carefully thought-out routine of Julia's numb life, when she receives a letter informing her that Mr Mackenzie's 'weekly allowance will be discontinued' (*ALM*, 14). This disruption in her well-ordered living death reintroduces time as process into her existence. Now she has to start planning again. It is then, as she is hurled into an active temporality, that the first image of an insubstantial world crops up: the pedestrians on the Boulevard Saint-Michel are likened to gesticulating shadows (*ALM*, 16). The dissolution of the world around her is perfected in London. The crossing of the Channel, induced by her desire to reconnect herself, leads her to a nebulous world peopled with disembodied creatures, ghosts 'melt[ing] away' or 'vague-looking people' (*ALM*, 50). The Channel, then, is a combination of the Lethe and of the Acheron. Crossing it means both to come out of oblivion, to plunge into active time, and to enter the kingdom of the dead and of a shapeless temporality.

Surprisingly enough, the shapeless time that conveys Julia's loss of direction is balanced against precise clockwork at the level of the narrating. The narrative constantly draws attention to its chronological joints but the nature of the various incidents thus rigorously situated in time tends to expose this clockwork as useless. Apart from the narrative's lavish use of time-markers, certain scenes are timed with what might appear as superfluous precision:

> Julia had not been in the restaurant for more than twelve minutes at the outside. (*ALM*, 27)

> In seven minutes she was ready. (*ALM*, 86)

Far from making for consistency and constructing Julia's life into a significant whole, these time-markers refract her disorientation and the haphazard arrangement of her petty occupations. Although they ensure continuity where form is concerned, they bring into relief the pathetic flatness of her disjointed life. This is particularly true of the third part of *After Leaving Mr Mackenzie*, in which Julia is again in Paris and is going through yet another interlude. Julia does not do much and yet the narrative ceaselessly marks out the hours:

> At lunch she drank a half-bottle of Burgundy and felt very hopeful. She spent the whole afternoon in the Galeries Lafayette choosing a dress and a hat. Then she went back to her hotel, dressed herself in her new clothes, and walked up and down her room, smoking. She decided that after dinner she would go to Montparnasse. She would go latish – between ten and eleven.

> At seven o'clock a gramophone started in a little
> café near by. [...]
> When she had finished dinner it was nearly nine
> o'clock. (*ALM*, 131–2)

The countdown leads nowhere really; it only makes
nothingness more accutely salient. Chronological jointing does not compensate for the disarticulation the trip
to London has brought into the open. This empty
clockwork cannot patch up the disoriented discontinuity
of Julia's biography. In the section entitled 'Childhood',
Julia proves unable to reconstruct chronology: '[t]he last
time you were happy about nothing; the first time you
were afraid about nothing. Which came first?'
(*ALM*, 116). Here the phrasing mirrors the loss of
articulation by bluntly juxtaposing noun clauses, while
the second-person mode points to the division of the
self. History does not provide linkage and, to support
this view, 'Childhood' starts with the following statement: '[e]very day is a new day. Every day you are a new
person' (*ALM*, 114). In the same way, Julia's trip to
London soon becomes 'a disconnected episode to be
placed with all the other disconnected episodes which
made up her life' (*ALM*, 129). Such acknowledgement of
disconnection ironically invalidates the chronological
ordering of the diegesis.

After Leaving Mr Mackenzie, then, displays a double
approach to time: precise chronology frames the representation of a life structured by disconnection and
juxtaposition. Pitted against each other, the two systems effect a laying-bare of devices: the text refers to a
model (chronological biography), while deconstructing
it through the demonstration that content is not
congruent with form. This coexistence is part of the
novel's resistance to closure. It is a way of modulating
the one-track quality of the narrative, of weaving

openness and possibility into the necessarily closed form of the work of art.

The Twilight Zone

The novel's resistance to closure makes way for what I shall call a twilight zone, where the woman's text unfolds. Apart from the fact that *After Leaving Mr Mackenzie* ends at the twilight hour of unreality – 'It was the hour between dog and wolf, as they say' (*ALM*, 138) – the trope can be useful as an expression of indeterminacy and transience. The twilight zone as I understand it is a borderline area between univocity or one-directional representation, materializing in the narrative's rigorous linearity or time-sequence, and indirection. *After Leaving Mr Mackenzie* is structured by a dialectic movement between closure and openness, an oscillation that becomes most dramatic in the last section of the book, aptly called 'Last'. In titling its last section 'Last', the text obviously claims its closure, all the more so as the section stages Julia's return to the Hôtel St Raphaël, the original diegetic setting. Here *After Leaving Mr Mackenzie* ostentatiously loops the loop, representing its own closure. On the other hand, the title of the novel, an unfinished sentence, as well as the last sentence, with its shadowy connotations, are both indicative of a desire for inconclusiveness. The markers of transience and indeterminacy compete with the markers of closure.

One aspect of this twilight zone is the way in which *After Leaving Mr Mackenzie* plays with the notion of irreversibility. The irreversible quality of the traditional plot is ironically challenged by the introduction of chance and unpredictability, notions which preside over Julia's existence. Julia is a fundamentally unpre-dictable character. Horsfield, for example, is puzzled by the unexpected turn things may take when Julia is involved. He is at a loss in front of reactions that simply cannot be accounted for. In a cinema, for example, Julia sheds embarrassing tears which could not have been brought about by the film they are watching (*ALM*, 34). Horsfield is even more surprised at Julia's unruffled air afterwards and ends up doubting whether she cried at all (*ALM*, 35). In 'The Staircase', Julia suddenly starts screaming, literally panic-stricken, simply because Horsfield overtook her without her realizing it (*ALM*, 118). This trifling incident has major consequences: it is more or less directly responsible for Julia's eviction, for the end of her relationship with Horsfield, followed by her departure from London. The effect is totally disproportionate to the cause. Generally speaking, Julia is a deviation from accepted paradigms, inviting those who come across her into a disquieting experience of defamiliarization. With Julia gone, Horsfield takes pleasure in the familiarity of his decent, diminutive environment,

> a world of lowered voices, and of passions, like Japanese dwarf trees, suppressed for many generations. A familiar world. (*ALM*, 127)

Julia's psychological unpredictability is replicated in the random way in which she lives her life. Chance rules her existence, in spite of the chronological arrangement of the plot. The last section stages a chance encounter with Mr Mackenzie, as if Jean Rhys wanted to make chance have the last word. Chance is also what prompts Julia to go to London:

> She thought: 'If a taxi hoots before I count three, I'll go to London. If not, I won't'. (*ALM*, 44)

The narrative still subscribes to traditional motivation: Julia's impulse to go to London can be rationalized in a number of ways. In the last analysis, however, as shown in this passage, a throw of the dice is what generates a new turn in the action. Chance is a parody of conventional causality. The poetics of indeterminacy which Jean Rhys elaborates necessarily violates the rules of verisimilitude – without wholly dismissing them – among which is the cause-and-effect relationship. Meant to hide the essential arbitrariness of any narrative, causality is here unmasked as a perfunctory contrivance.

Part of this exposure is the suggestion of an essential reversibility. A good deal of dithering precedes any action Julia takes and once the decision is made, as in the case of her decision to go to London, it proves to be reversible: '[a]ll the time she packed she was thinking: "After all, I haven't taken my ticket yet. I needn't go if I don't want to"' (*ALM*, 44–5). Thus the narrative deconstructs its own irreversibility. While fulfilling the conditions of verisimilitude and intelligibility – Jean Rhys never departs from realism – *After Leaving Mr Mackenzie* breaks the causal mould by suggesting that the story could at any time take another line of action. It designates the freedom, common to all narratives, of taking whatever course at whatever time, an arbitrariness that plot consistency is meant to screen. In *After Leaving Mr Mackenzie*, anyway, choices are not made once for all. Similarly, things are subjected to several – sometimes conflicting – evaluations. Plurality is one of the weapons against closure. Jean Rhys makes use of variable internal focalization, for example. Most of the characters are focal characters at some stage, thus pluralizing perception and truth. Moreover, the same event may be focused through several characters, multiple focalization conferring on the scene an ever-fluctuating meaning. The scene in the Restaurant Albert where Julia slaps Mr Mackenzie's face (*ALM*, 22–6) is alternately focused through Mr Mackenzie – with occasional insights into Albert's perception of it – and Horsfield, who happens to have dinner in the same restaurant. Although the two perspectives do not diverge radically – Julia's perspective might have shed a radically different light on the incident – the reader must take up two problematical views of reality instead of a single unquestioned one. The modulations at work in multiple focalization cause things to appear 'as in an unstill pool of water', as Horsfield puts it (*ALM*, 28).

As well as introducing alternative points of view, *After Leaving Mr Mackenzie* sketches out alternatives to its own plot. Some of them remain embryonic. On three occasions, for example, Julia is approached by unknown men, which creates the possibility of a different diegetic destiny. None of these chance encounters develops into anything significant, but they introduce virtuality in the novel. After all, Julia met Horsfield in just the same way; elaborating on these brief encounters rather than on Horsfield might have led to a completely different narrative. These incipient relationships are all the more significant as they coincide with turning-points in the novel. The first encounter occurs just before Julia leaves for London (*ALM*, 45), the second one after her mother's death and her fight with Norah (*ALM*, 102), the last one as, back in Paris, Julia is trying to regain some sense of direction (*ALM*, 135). At each of its turning-points, the novel exhibits the range of possibilities it could have exploited, although, for the sake of readability, it regretfully selects only one. The first and last of these encounters are respectively included in the sections entitled 'The First Unknown' and 'The Second Unknown', two resting-places or transitional sections in which, by definition, anything might happen. The tightness of the plot is shaken.

The sustaining of possibility within the closely knit plot is also afforded by the delineation of potential series. Two sections in Part Two, 'It Might Have Happened Anywhere' and 'The Staircase', constitute a kind of couplet in the sense that they stage two similar scenes, whose outcome is nonetheless very different. Both are set in the Notting Hill boarding-house and in both sections, Horsfield and Julia tiptoe up the stairs to Julia's room on the sly, for men are not allowed in at night. In the first case, their illegal ascent towards Julia's room leads to the consummation of the relationship. In the second case, despite analogous circumstances, the ascent takes a tragic turn: because Julia is suddenly panic-stricken in the dark, her relationship with Horsfield comes to a premature end. The duplication of the scene demonstrates that a trifling mishap is all that is needed to upset dramatically the course of events. The finality of the plot is precarious and, to the end, the novel claims that 'anything might happen' (*ALM*, 131).

'Anything might happen': the phrase epitomizes the resistance of *After Leaving Mr Mackenzie* to finite representation. Through the twilight zone that blurs univocal perceptions and defeats definite labelling, the novel constantly points to the possible, while actualizing the plausible. Incomplete and unpredictable, Julia Martin is a heroine whose characterization gradually reaches a certain degree of completion, but no revelation occurs. She stands somewhere between semantic fullness and indeterminacy, 'between dog and wolf'. *After Leaving Mr Mackenzie* is thus an ambiguous novel creating the conditions for the emergence of a woman's text. *Quartet* is not devoid of ambiguity – in fact, no work of art is – but it fights off ambiguity by a saturating type of writing that seeks to joint, to link, to ensure the continuity of meaning, in order to convey a finite picture of the heroine. In *After Leaving Mr Mackenzie*, on the other hand, ambiguity and discontinuity become the very stuff of Jean Rhys's writing. The twilight zone, which does not quite allow for the emergence of a female voice, is dissidence. Incompleteness as resistance to closure and semantic instability create the possibility of a different mode of articulation, that still remains to be heard. What *After Leaving Mr Mackenzie* contributes to the woman's text is the idea that feminine discourse is to be found in the margins of any construct, of any discursive practice. The feminine is an elusive presence that Jean Rhys cannot quite articulate, but which she strives to recapture.

4 The Ironic Other

Sexual difference is structured by a binary system, one of whose terms, almost invariably the masculine one, is always privileged. In *The Second Sex*,[1] Simone de Beauvoir describes this binary system as the duality of Self and Other. Societies, she argues, are organized on the assumption that man is self and woman other, the consequences being always deleterious to women. This conception of alterity is echoed by Shoshana Felman, for example: '[t]heoretically subordinated to the concept of masculinity, the woman is viewed by man as *his* opposite, that is to say, as *his* other, the negative of the positive, and not, in her own right, different, other, Otherness itself'.[2] Woman then tends to be constructed negatively in an androcentric society. She is defined by what she lacks and enters history with a piece missing. Such conception of an incomplete other subordinated to a masculine self is the point of departure of Luce Irigaray's *Spéculum de l'autre femme*.[3] In her reading of Freud's lecture on femininity, she points out that, for Freud, sexual difference comes down to the simple fact that the male has an obvious sex organ, not the female. Female difference is then perceived as an absence or the negative of the male norm. Woman is not only the other but man's other, his negative or mirror-image, man's specularized other which has meaning only in relation to him. 'Caught in the specular logic of patriarchy, woman can choose either to remain silent, producing incomprehensible babble (any utterance that falls outside the logic of the same will by definition be incomprehensible to the male master discourse) or to enact the specular representation of herself as a lesser male.'[4]

Unable to articulate the feminine outside the logic of the same, Jean Rhys, on the face of it, posits woman as man's other. Although her fiction is ostensibly haunted by this specularized other, we shall see that she manages to turn otherness into an active pole. Far from being the specularized icon of subordination to masculine discourse, otherness features as a deregulating machinery used to question the ipseity and legitimacy of the patriarchal system.

Foreign Bodies

In Jean Rhys's novels or short fiction, the heroines are invariably placed in surroundings with which they are not familiar and where they emerge as foreign bodies. In 'Let Them Call It Jazz',[5] for instance, the narrator is a young West Indian half-breed who speaks broken English with occasional incursions into Creole. Thanks to this foregrounding of a linguistic other breaking grammatical laws, otherness weaves itself into the very substance of the text. Displaced into a uniform and respectable suburban area, Selina Davis stands out as somebody radically different, disrupting uniformity, which as such constitutes a subversion. Her behaviour is moreover unacceptable by suburban standards: she drinks, sings at the top of her voice in her garden, calls her neighbours names and is a kept woman. The alien has to be subdued and is sent to prison. In 'Overture and Beginners Please',[6] a young girl arrives in England which, as it soon turns out, is to be the locus of a painful apprenticeship. Again, the heroine's otherness is foregrounded as she bears the name of her native land, 'West Indies'. In Jean Rhys's stories, the representation of otherness often combines phallocentrism and ethnocentrism.

The novels, whether they are set in Paris, London or the West Indies, are equally concerned with otherness. Wherever they come from, the heroines are all strangers or foreigners forever in transit, forever not belonging, staying in hotel rooms which they never make theirs. Not quite homeless but of no fixed abode, they are exiles, which is the characteristic condition of what Julia Kristeva calls 'l'étranger'.[7] Having no known destination, they also seem to come from nowhere. In an attempt to disentangle otherness from specularization, Jean Rhys tends to cloud the issue of the heroines' origins, as if she sought to shift the emphasis on to 'Otherness itself'. Mentioning their nationality or origin does not create any sense of belonging. Roots in Jean Rhys's fiction are something you are forever cut off from, something you never return to. In *Quartet*, Marya Zelli, who is characterized by 'a lack of solidity and of fixed background' (*Q*, 14), finds it difficult to persuade Heidler that she is English. To come from somewhere so definite and so recognizable as England is out of character. Married to a Pole, himself an exile, Marya is even incapable of becoming integrated into the cosmopolitan world of the Parisian Left Bank. In *After Leaving Mr Mackenzie*, Julia Martin is also an Englishwoman in Paris and has a South American mother. As soon as it is spelled out however, her origin seems to recede again: her mother, a generally 'inarticulate' woman (*ALM*, 76), is not inclined to speak of her native country. On the other hand, returning to England, Julia's place of birth, is made impossible by age-old family conflicts. In *Good Morning Midnight*, Sasha's nationality is exhibited by her clothes – 'it shouts "Anglaise", my hat' (*GMM*, 14) – and, in the eyes of a shop assistant, she is 'a strange client, l'étrangère' (*GMM*, 59). Apart from this, however, little is known of her past: a few phrases such as 'the old devil' or bare pronouns with no antecedents (*GMM*, 36) suggest a past scarred with conflicts and rejections that forbid any return to England and signify uprooting more than roots.

'Sasha' is in fact the name that the heroine chose for herself – her real name is Sophia (*GMM*, 37) – trying to break away from genealogy and to sever herself from her origins. Changing her name, which, Sasha feels, might change her luck (*GMM*, 11), is a Promethean way of giving birth to herself, of creating her destiny. Bypassing the law of the father, usurping the power of naming, Sasha seeks to become other, as opposed to man's specularized other. Her life, however, suggests that, whatever she does, there is no escaping the logic of the same. In 'Till September Petronella',[8] changing one's name denotes the same desire to sever oneself from one's roots: '[i]f you knew how bloody my home was you wouldn't be surprised that I wanted to change my name and forget all about it' (*Tigers*, 15). The heroines do not always go as far as changing their names but identity is often problematized in Jean Rhys's fiction. In 'Let Them Call It Jazz', Selina Davis, we are told, bears the name of her father. However, she immediately qualifies the statement by saying that her father was 'a first-class liar' and that she is not even sure that 'Davis' is his real name (*Tigers*, 15). By questioning the reliability of names and by generally loosening family ties, Jean Rhys might seek to represent obliquely 'Otherness itself', woman 'in her own right'.

Voyage in the Dark also places difference 'in its own right' at centre-stage. Anna Morgan comes from the West Indies but where she comes from is hardly relevant, as the nickname the other chorus girls give her, 'the Hottentot', suggests (*VD*, 12). What matters is Anna's essential difference, a difference that seems to be considered outside the duality of self and other. Anna's arrival in England is to be understood as a second birth altogether: '[i]t was as if a curtain had fallen, hiding everything I had ever known. It was almost like being born again' (*VD*, 7). A curtain comes to screen Anna's origin, making her *dépaysement* complete. Strangers rather than foreigners, Jean Rhys's women belong to another space or a space that is other. Her ambition is to have them stand 'outside the machine', to borrow from the title of one of her stories. Such is indeed the stance of Inez in 'Outside the Machine'.[9] Lying in her hospital bed, she is on the margin, outside the flow of daily life as well as estranged from hospital routine, its smooth mechanism and well-ordered component parts:

> [The nurses] moved about surely and quickly. They did everything in an impersonal way. They were like parts of a machine, she thought, that was working smoothly. The women in the beds bobbed up and down and in and out. They too were parts of a machine. (*Tigers*, 82)

Contrary to those patients who are 'parts of a machine', Inez is heterogeneous: '[b]ecause she was outside the machine they might come along any time with a pair of huge iron tongs and pick her up and put her on the rubbish heap, and there she would lie and rot' (*Tigers*, 82). Inez's heterogeneity or exterritoriality – she is 'out of place' (*Tigers*, 80) – is pitted against perfectly integrated, 'aggressively respectable' women (*Tigers*, 80), whose discourse is riddled with common-places and reflects consensual taxonomy:

> 'An English person? English, what sort of English? To which of the seven divisions, sixty-nine subdivisions, and thousand-and-three subsubdivisions do you belong?' (*Tigers*, 81)

Inez belongs to none and cannot be categorized. She is otherness.

Disentangling otherness from specularization can only be an attempt, an ambition that Jean Rhys could only achieve by emancipating herself from discourse, thus producing 'incomprehensible babble'. All she can do is to problematize the polarity of self and other or to represent her heroines as exiles, divorced from their origin, consistently heterogeneous, 'out of place'. Another option is to make this necessarily specularized otherness productive. Thus, from the representation of the feminine as other, Jean Rhys moves to the examination of the interaction of the foreign body with 'the machine'. The confrontation creates an ironic reshuffling of categories: from the perspective of the alien, the system itself becomes alien, cryptic and illegitimate.

Defamiliarization

The feminine is to be heard in this shift of perspective. The stranger's gaze displaces strangeness. From her point of view, otherness becomes immanent to the codes regulating the patriarchal community. Like the work of art, the stranger 'removes objects from the automatism of perception'.[10] Once removed from the straitjacket of routine, the various codings that cement the community appear incongruous as well as ridiculous. The feminine is then the vehicle of satire.

This shift of perspective is most apparent in one of the short stories, 'The Day They Burnt the Books'.[11] The story is set in the West Indies, with England featuring as *l'ailleurs*. Seen from the Caribbean, that distant, 'mysterious, obscure and sacred' place (*Tigers*, 38) that the West Indians of English descent call home, is not devoid of a bizarre dimension:

It was Eddie [. . .] who first infected me with doubts about 'home', meaning England. He would be quiet when others who had never seen it – none of us had ever seen it – were talking about its delights, gesticulating freely as we talked – London, the beautiful, rosy-cheeked ladies, the theatres, the shops, the fog, the blazing coal fires in winter, the exotic food (whitebait eaten to the sound of violins), strawberries and cream – the word 'strawberries' always spoken with a guttural and throaty sound which we imagined to be the proper English pronunciation. (*Tigers*, 38–9)

English culture now features as a foreign body with its 'exotic food' and strange uses. The best illustration of its heterogeneity is perhaps the library of Mr Sawyer, the father of the narrator's friend, who, we are told, hates everything about the Caribbean. His library, full of imported books ranging from the *Encyclopaedia Britannica* to Milton's and Byron's poems, has been added on to the back of the house as if British culture could not be directly assimilated into the West Indian milieu. Although Eddie claims ownership of this awkward extension after his father's death – ' "My room", Eddie called it. "My books", he would say, "My books" '. (*Tigers*, 40) – his coloured mother does not deem this legacy suitable. She gleefully burns her late husband's misplaced books which, to her, are a symbol of imperialist oppression. Her hateful revenge, however, does not eradicate imperial culture altogether: two books are rescued, Kipling's *Kim* and Maupassant's *Fort comme la mort*, 'representing the two imperial cultures to which the children are inheritors'.[12] Their surviving Mrs Sawyer's auto-da-fé indicates 'the survival of a literary tradition, though within the compromised circumstances of colonial inheritance'.[13]

For a colonial, life in England, a country both familiar
and strange, requires a certain amount of apprenticeship. Living in the 'home country' inevitably takes the
shape of an exploration of the unknown and the
stranger inevitably assumes the function of an interpreter and a decipherer. The opacity of the excessively
obscure codes the stranger comes up against is part of
the satire. Apprenticeship contributes little to the
betterment of the heroine's condition as it tends to do
in the *Bildungsroman*. It is most of the time represented
as alienation. In *Good Morning Midnight*, for example,
Sasha ironically sees hair-dyeing, a fairly violent process
implying bleaching before another colour is imposed
upon the denatured hair, as an apt metaphor for
apprenticeship (*GMM*, 44). In 'Let Them Call It Jazz',
Selina Davis has to go through the brainwashing
experience of imprisonment before she understands
English rites. Before she becomes acceptable by English
standards, she must become a stranger to herself:
'there's a small looking glass in my cell and I see
myself and I'm like somebody else. Like some strange
new person' (*Tigers*, 60). By the end of her time in jail,
she has become familiar with the rules and is, for
instance, able to make conversation in a satisfactory way:

> At the station I'm waiting for the train and a woman
> asks if I feel well. 'You look so tired', she says. 'Have
> you come a long way?' I want to answer, 'I come so
> far I lose myself on that journey'. But I tell her, 'Yes, I
> am quite well. But I can't stand the heat'. She says she
> can't stand it either, and we talk about the weather till
> the train come in. (*Tigers*, 62)

One of the things that Selina has learnt is that discussing
the weather, a commonplace in the literal sense of the
word, is preferable to exhibiting one's unspeakable

otherness. What Selina has learnt is compromise and dissembling, and this is how she manages to find a job: 'I lie and tell them I work in very expensive New York shop. I speak bold and smooth faced, and they never check up on me' (*Tigers*, 62–3).

In 'Let Them Call It Jazz', Selina's apprenticeship is quite successful. By the end of the story, she manages to intervene in her new surroundings and gains control over her life. This does not mean, however, that her education results in perfect adhesion to the system. There is always a critical distance, as the phrasing of the title of the story suggests, pinpointing the unbridgeable gap that separates the heroine's discourse from that of the community, from consensual discourse. 'Jazz' is what the others call 'the Holloway song' that Selina heard in prison. Like the trumpets of Jericho, the singular, subversive song is capable of pulling walls down and of showing the way towards some Promised Land: 'it don't fall down and die in the courtyard; seems to me it could jump the gates of the jail easily and travel far, and nobody could stop it' (*Tigers*, 60). The song, opens up a private space where difference can express itself. Selina is soon to be deprived of her wondrous song, however, as a man she meets at a party jazzes it up and sells it. Instead of weeping over her dispossession, Selina spends the £5 he sent her for her contribution on a pink dress – the apprenticeship of compromise is successfully completed. Although the final lines are ambiguous, one has the feeling that the Holloway song is a major breakthrough in Selina's development:

> Even if they played it on trumpets, even if they played it just right, like I wanted – no walls would fall so soon. 'So let them call it jazz', I think, and let them play it wrong. That won't make no difference to the song I heard. (*Tigers*, 63)

This can be read in two ways: she either means that the defiant song she heard was useless anyway, or that she will never be entirely deprived of it. She has been radically transformed by it – she was a victim, she is now a survivor – and while fulfilling the requirements of social existence, she is still possessed of her dissident difference.

The outcome is not always as successful as in 'Let Them Call It Jazz', even when advisers or guides help the heroine along with the educating process. In 'A Solid House',[14] for instance, the protagonist returns to normality under the aegis of a guide, Mrs Spearman, her lodger. The latter readily imparts some of her worldly-wise knowledge of the female condition to Teresa:

> Of course, it's better to be calm. I don't believe in hysteria. Not for women, anyhow. Sometimes a man can get away with hysteria, but not a woman. And then of course don't be too much alone. People don't like it. The things they say if you're alone! You have to have a good deal of money to get away with that. And keep up with your friends. Write letters. And a good laugh always helps, of course. (*Tigers*, 123)

In *Voyage in the Dark*, Anna is surrounded by well-meaning advisers who teach her 'etiquette', that is, how to behave with men or what to say when, for instance, one is asked out by a man for the first time: '("Always say you have a previous engagement")' (*VD*, 17). Throughout the novel, Anna conscientiously recites to herself the principles she is being taught: '(A lady always puts on her gloves before going into the street)' (*VD*, 30). As is the case here, they are most of the time bracketed or italicized as if they had been grafted on to Anna's narrative. Anna, it seems, simply cannot assimilate these teachings, which are made to feature as an alien text, an ironically inverted reflection of her own estrangement and maladjustment.

Generally speaking, the heroines put in quite a lot of energy and effort to understand, decipher and conform to the prevailing codes. Acquiring technical know-how, a more specific form of social know-how, is often one of their main concerns, and it always proves difficult: '[Marya] learned, after long and painstaking effort, to talk like a chorus girl, to dress like a chorus girl and to think like a chorus girl – up to a point' (Q, 15). The final modulating addition 'up to a point' is emblematic of the residual, defamiliarizing distance that always separates the trainee from the various codings. The same distance appears in Sasha's retrospective outlook when she looks back on the often ludicrously obscure codes of the various jobs she had. Once an assistant in a shop symptomatically called 'Young Britain', she was puzzled and eventually defeated by the cryptic system of the cash-register: 'X plus ZBW. That meant fcs. 68–60. Then another hieroglyphic – XQ15tn – meant something else, fcs. 112-75' (GMM, 26). Although one may have the feeling that Sasha is being victimized by such complex codes (she gets the sack from Young Britain), excessive opacity makes the system ridiculous. Of course the heroine fails in her apprenticeship, but her failure is above all a sharp commentary on the ludicrous opacity that caused it. The cipher of the cash-register is a metonymy for the tacit codings that regulate society, and apprenticeship, in Jean Rhys's texts is used as an opportunity of carrying out, through the eyes of the stranger, a critical evaluation of the norm. The education process necessarily induces a comparison between the norm and the heterogeneous element, a comparison that proves deleterious to the norm more than to the heterogeneous element. Decentring the norm is the source of much irony and this is how Jean Rhys turns the other, this subordinated entity, into a subversive force. From the point of view of the other, the norm itself becomes other.

Irony, or the Rhetoric of the Feminine

Foreign bodies in Jean Rhys's work do not provide role-models. Jean Rhys does not seek to disparage some laws to promote others. There is no such thing as certainty or assertive knowledge in her fiction. Her texts are, then, not quite satiric for, according to Linda Hutcheon, satire tends to be ameliorative in its intention; it possesses 'a scornful or disdainful ethos', but 'should not be confused with simple invective [...] for the corrective aim of satire's scornful ridicule is central to its identity. While satire can be destructive, there is also an implied idealism.'[15] Reference to such ideal, whether stated or implied, is not to be found in Jean Rhys's texts. The foreign body is therefore less satiric than the vehicle of irony, whose ethos is 'a mocking one',[16] a simply pejorative one. Thus, if the critical gaze of '*l'étrangère*' is generally non-prescriptive, it creates dissonance and introduces relativity and polyphony into the self-legitimizing monolith of the norm.

Otherness and irony have structural common points. This community of structure has been underlined by Linda Hutcheon, who establishes a parallel between irony (and parody), and Shklovsky's 'defamiliarization'.[17] The foreign body serves as a deviating device, thanks to which what is familiar seems new, as if perceived for the first time. Likewise, irony as a trope constitutes a deviation from the norm, a deviation that sheds a new light on the norm, makes it appear other.

Through the figure of the stranger, irony, verbal or situational, pervades the whole text, determining both selection of fictional material and structure. Such pervasive use of irony can easily be accounted for. It is all at once congruent with Jean Rhys's oppositional stance, with her taste for expressive restraint and with the feminine idiom as a silent yet alternative one.

Recent studies of irony place the emphasis on its pragmatic value. 'Irony judges', says Linda Hutcheon: '[t]he pragmatic function of irony is one of signalling evaluation, most frequently of a pejorative nature'.[18] Through irony, Jean Rhys gives a silent and nonetheless powerful voice to protest or dissidence. On the semantic level, ironic utterances rest on antiphrasis, an opposition between an intended and a stated meaning, the marking of difference being achieved by means of superimposition of semantic contexts. To be specifically ironic, this semantic doubling must be combined with a reshuffling of 'normal' semantic hierarchy: the inferred, latent meaning is foregrounded at the expense of the stated meaning. Difference and the unspoken are, then, given pride of place in the ironic mode, all the more so as, Beda Allemann argues, the degree of ironic effect in a text is inversely proportionate to the number of overt signals needed to achieve that effect. If the lack of signals makes the decoding of irony uncertain, the ironist is, on the other hand, a kind of 'funambulist', as Beda Allemann puts it, who must be clear without being obvious, say something without actually saying it, strike a balance between excessive discretion and ostentation.[19] The feminine, itself other and unspeakable, may then find in irony and its unspoken rhetoric an opportunity of making itself heard. Thanks to irony, Jean Rhys finds a way of altering the stereotype of the silenced woman: the Rhys woman may well be silenced, but hers is an active, productive form of silence.

Antiphrasis

The fundamental semantic antiphrasis in Jean Rhys's fiction consists of staging a set of androcentric, consensual norms while showing that what is usually taken as 'civilized' or 'proper' behaviour is in fact akin to primitive barbarity. In her texts, the norm is a kind of diffuse menace and is usually endowed with incredible violence. The representatives of this atopic threat form a faceless crowd, sometimes referred to by an amorphous 'they', and propriety often flakes off to unveil a debased humanity, a world of predators ready to swoop down on whoever stands outside consensus. The Heidlers are such predators and the violence one may observe in *Quartet* permeates many of Jean Rhys's texts. 'Till September Petronella', for instance, is structured upon another 'quartet', four characters renting a cottage in the countryside. Soon enough, the supposedly peaceful atmosphere of a holiday in the country deteriorates. The relationship between the four protagonists is rather strained, tension within the cottage being aggravated by tension without. The local people hate them for some obscure reason; it seems that, as a rule, 'the ruddy citizens' (*Tigers*, 18) just hate the heterogeneous. Frankie, one of the characters, voices this unmotivated hostility:

> 'We've only been here a fortnight, but they've got up a hate you wouldn't believe'. (*Tigers*, 12)

> 'They'll kick your face to bits if you let them. And shriek with laughter at the damage'. (*Tigers*, 13)

Their stay is indeed interspersed with violent rows, between a local farmer and Marston and Petronella, who were only looking at his field (*Tigers*, 17), or between Marston and a passenger on a bus (*Tigers*, 20).

More generally, this diffuse hatred materializes in the metaphor of a glaring light that irresistibly floods the scene, persecuting the inmates of the cottage: '[a] hot, white glare shone in our eyes. We tried pulling the blinds down, but one got stuck and we went on eating in the glare' (*Tigers*, 18). The same harassing glare, a metaphor for atopic aggression and malevolence, reappears in other stories, in 'A Solid House' in particular:

> It was a glittering, glaring day outside, the sky blown blue. A heartless, early spring day – acid, like an unripe gooseberry. There was a cold yellow light on the paved garden and the tidy, empty flower beds and on the high wall, where a ginger cat sat staring at birds. (*Tigers*, 120)

Latent violence is part and parcel of the peacefulness of the surroundings, where orderly flower beds and predatory cats coalesce. Anyway, this quiet garden is but incidental in the story whose backdrop is the Second World War. The context of the Blitz lends an insight into the 'natural' relationship between androcentric society and violence. War is legitimate violence, and in licit warfare, civilization exhibits its fundamental barbarity.

The 'solid house' stands in contrapuntal relation to the chaos of war striking two streets away from it. It is this anachronic haven of peace that Jean Rhys chooses to throw light in an ironic way on to the norm's barbaric uses. The house itself is an oxymoronic combination of savagery and civilization, war and peace. Two antonymic signifieds coexist, the stated one (peace and propriety) receding before the unspoken one (violence). Civilization materializes in phenomena that the text obliquely designates as merely perfunctory. On the face of it, Miss Spearman, for instance, is the epitome of the respectable

landlady – a species which Jean Rhys is always highly
suspicious of. Yet Miss Spearman is a living antiphrasis:
her sweetness is ironically challenged by her rather
phallic name with a definite military ring to it.[20] The
(latent) war lord lies dormant in the (stated) sweet
landlady and the war lord surfaces whenever Miss
Spearman loses her temper, momentarily oblivious of
propriety. She claims, for instance, that she hired her
cleaning lady 'for love' (*Tigers*, 119), thus contributing
something to the betterment of the working class. The
reader still has her professed philanthropy in mind
when, a few pages later, Miss Spearman flares up:

> 'Was that the bell?' Miss Spearman sat very erect.
> 'It's that slut Nelly. Excuse the word. Over two hours
> late'.
>   She went out into the hall, and Nelly could be
> heard, loudly explaining, arguing, and then becom-
> ing aggressive. And Miss Spearman's shrill answers,
> which ended on a high, thin note. (*Tigers*, 124)

Here verbal violence 'accidentally' contradicts Miss
Spearman's earlier compassion, but even when she
manages to remain ladylike and lives up to the prescriptions of middle-class propriety, violence seems to be part
of her daily routine: '[s]he lit the fire, talking about air
raids, land mines and slaughter' (*Tigers*, 115). In the same
way, she is eager to take a look at the damage caused by
the latest air raid, such morbid sightseeing providing
occasion for a little stroll (*Tigers*, 117).

The house itself is subjected to the same antiphrastic
strategy. Clean, cosy, quiet, it nonetheless accommo-
dates former officers who, although too old to be
dangerous, signify that the 'solid house' may not be
immune to warfare and destruction. The subdued
atmosphere, the 'old prints of soldiers in full dress'

(*Tigers*, 115) and the tenants' distinguished demeanour cannot quite alleviate the horror of the slaughter outside. Worse still, they might be seen as a doubling of outer havoc. When Captain Roper, one of Miss Spearman's tenants, tells his life story to Teresa, he does not mention heroic feats of arms, as one might have expected, but tells the heroine how, after the First World War, he gave mah-jong lessons in an attempt to survive global wreckage. Captain Roper's tale, in form as well as content, fails to counteract the disintegration of meaning subsequent to wartime chaos; it reflects chaos, listing dates in a disorderly manner to an absent-minded addressee whose abstraction contributes to emptying his narrative of meaning:

> Teresa stopped listening. When she next heard what he was saying he was no longer in 1914; he was in 1924, giving lessons in Mah Jong to keep body and soul together.
> [...] 'I'll never know the rest of the story – what happened in 1925 or 1938, in 1927 or 1931...'
> (*Tigers*, 116–17)

In just the same way as Captain Roper's disconnected autobiography ironically fails to 'keep body and soul together', the house is an ironic reflection of what is taking place outside. The casualties of the morning's bombings have indoor counterparts, stuffed birds 'neatly labelled in careful, slanting handwriting', equipped with a most ironic caption in the same handwriting: 'I believe in the Resurrection of the Dead' (*Tigers*, 125). Given the context, and in spite of this hopeful motto, the birds are far removed from being phoenixes, and taxidermy connects with Miss Spearman's fascination for the morbid more than with her faith in life after death.

The ironic commingling of consensus and violence is also suggested by the fact that the story functions as a kind of echo-chamber. Through the protagonist's interior monologue, reference is made to previous wreckage. Violence is not limited to the confines of the 'solid house' and its neighbourhood. There was once another solid house, as Teresa's mental text tells us: '[t]he other was solid, too' (*Tigers*, 121). Like the eponymous house, the other one is marred with images of death, the description eliciting dereliction rather than solidity:

> The water was covered with dead leaves. The paddle did not make any sound, the dead leaves slowed the punt down. Round the corner was the house [...]. It looked empty and dilapidated. The boards of the landing-stage were broken and rotten. (*Tigers*, 122).

As well as undermining stated solidity, decay and rot connote the deadly dimension of the norm and the violence of the other's eviction. We are given to understand that Teresa was once denied admission to that house, which led her to suicide. When the story starts, Teresa is just about recovering and trying to gain admission to an equally deadly universe which, strangely enough, now welcomes her. The reason for such a belated admission may be that, the Second World War serving as a sufficient outlet for its immanent barbarity, the community's violence no longer needs a scapegoat.

The story, then, constantly moves from the particular to the general, suggesting that violence is ubiquitous, within and without, past and present. The system of echoes on which it is based encapsulates the way in which irony is produced. As we saw, the ironic trope is devoid of overt signals but signals must perforce exist within the text in order to allow the decoder to pick up the encoder's ironic intent. To account for the paradoxical nature of the ironic signal – unobtrusive and yet perceptible – Dan Sperber and Deirdre Wilson argue that most ironies function as implicit mentions.[21] Ironic utterances implicitly echo an utterance which is the object of negative evaluation. Thus in 'A Solid House', the foregrounded house is in fact the echo of a backgrounded house elliptically referred to in Teresa's interior monologue, the mention altering meaning in the process. It indeed calls for a reassessment of the adjective 'solid', for instance. If, at first sight, Miss Spearman's house stands out as a reassuring stronghold against a background of global disintegration, it undergoes a covert metamorphosis in the course of the story, becoming one of the icons of violence. Jean Rhys starts with a patent dichotomy between war and peace and gradually equates domestic peace with ruthless strife. This implicit equation is supported by another echo, as Teresa takes shelter in Miss Spearman's cellar during an air-raid. There she remembers another cellar where she used to play, along with other children. Before long, the children's harmless game of hide-and-seek takes on a warlike dimension:

> The boys showed off, became brutal; the girls trotted along, imitating, trying to keep up, but with sidelong looks, sudden fits of giggling, which often ended in tears. [...]
> 'Nothing changes much', she thought, remembering the bellowed orders, contradicted the next minute – Left turn. No, right turn. No, as you were, silly ass – the obligatory grin, the idiotic jokes, repeated over and over again, which you had to laugh at, at first unwillingly, then so hysterically that your jaws ached, and the endless arguments as to whether the girls might carry knives slung to their waists or not. (*Tigers*, 113–14)

Lord of the Flies comes to mind. This passage exhibits – in a fairly unironic way – the androcentric barbarity that turns girls into either aping collaborators or victims. Of course, normal violence overlaps the male/female dichotomy: trying to become integrated into the norm, Jean Rhys tells us, comes down to joining 'the noble and gallant army of witch-hunters – both sexes, all ages eligible – so eagerly tracking down some poor devil, snouts to the ground' (*Tigers*, 123). Contrary to the previous passage, this sentence is definitely ironic: it includes two metaphors bringing close together two contrasting isotopies, chivalry and bestiality. Such semantic contrast is the signal of the ironic ethos of the story.

Hyperbolic irony

In exposing the latent violence of the peaceful or the hidden barbarity of the civilized through ironic anti-phrasis, Jean Rhys may at times sound moralistic or Manichaean. Rhysian antiphrasis belongs to Wayne C. Booth's category of 'stable irony'. Although covert, the intended meaning is easily reconstructed and offers a sound basis for subverting the surface meaning: '[t]he meanings are hidden, but when they are discovered by the proper reader they are firm as a rock'.[22] Here Jean Rhys is closest to satire. Sometimes, however, 'no stable reconstruction can be made out of the ruins revealed through the irony'.[23] Such is the case when ironic effect is derived from hyperbole. The stance of the encoder is then less 'ameliorative'; he or she refuses to declare himself or herself for any stable proposition. In Jean Rhys's poetics, hyperbolic irony partakes of a more negative ethos with no secure evaluative standpoint. By ironic hyperbole I designate a number of devices, ranging from exaggeration to oversimplification, that all say more while meaning less, thus preserving the co-presence of two semantic levels necessary to the creation of irony.

Hyperbolic distortion can be traced in a recurrent synecdoche, a sneer which the heroines come up against and which, like the harrowing glare discussed earlier, stands for anonymous malevolence. Disembodied and proliferating, the sneer is the 'ruddy citizens'' response to difference. In 'Till September Petronella', the heroine manages to hold it at bay by claiming membership of a fashionable club. This shallow token of conformity is enough to make her one of the fold and to defuse her interlocutor's sneer:

> I had touched the right spring – even the feeling of his hand on my arm changed. *Always the same spring to touch before the sneering expression will go out of their eyes and the sneering sound out of their voices*. (*Tigers*, 32)

In *Voyage in the Dark*, however, Anna Morgan is not familiar enough with the codes of social intercourse to be able to neutralize that evil smile. She meets it everywhere she goes, especially when the code of dress is violated: 'it's jaw, jaw and sneer, sneer all the time. And the shop-windows sneering and smiling in your face' (*VD*, 22). Anna's otherness is met by the same sneer in Walter Jeffries's house, the icon of respectability, 'sneering faintly, sneering discreetly, as a servant would' (*VD*, 43).

Occasionally, this scornful smile is hyperbolically distorted into grotesque laughter, deactivating horror with a touch of ridicule. In 'A Solid House', for example, the harassing anonymous representatives of the norm are made innocuous by hyperbole and Teresa's supreme detachment:

> If they were to laugh until their mouths met at the
> back and the tops of their heads fell off like some
> loathsome over-ripe fruit as they doubtless will one
> day you wouldn't turn your head to see the horrible
> but comic sight... (*Tigers*, 122)

The nightmarish vision of people's cruelty is downgraded into a laughable sight. Resting on the combination of frightful and ludicrous features, the grotesque
effects deflation: hyperbolic distortion results in 'hypo-
bolic' meaning. If grotesque defamiliarization exhibits
the demoniac component of the norm, laughter eventually defuses its evil power by exposing its meaninglessness.

Most of the time, this distortion-plus-neutralization is
effected by means of a bestiary, a good sample of which is
to be found in 'Tigers Are Better-Looking'.[24] The story
starts with a note explaining why Hans, a friend of the
protagonist's, is leaving London: 'I got the feeling that I
was surrounded by a pack of timid tigers waiting to
spring the moment anybody is in trouble or hasn't any
money. *But tigers are better-looking, aren't they?*' (*Tigers*, 64;
original emphasis). The oxymoron 'timid tigers' evokes a
hybrid creature, between the awesome majesty of the
tiger and the aggressiveness of the coward. This hybrid
might also be a parody of the 'fearful symmetry' of
Blake's 'tyger'. Blake's adjective, 'fearful', which celebrates the beauty of evil, is ironically replaced by 'timid':
Jean Rhys's second-rate tigers are frightened rather than
frightening. Thanks to ironic hyperbole, we paradoxically move a step down 'the Great Chain of Being' on
many occasions. The divine is downgraded into the
human in a small ad in which some angry individual
impersonates God and divine wrath[25] while the human is
downgraded into the bestial: '*Faces, faces, faces.... Like
hyenas, like swine, like goats, like apes, like parrots. But not*

tigers, because tigers are better-looking, aren't they?' (*Tigers*, 69; original emphasis). Again the various similes refer to animals which consistently come short of feline gracefulness and can only 'ape' the injuring power of tigers.

In *Voyage in the Dark*, the synecdoche of the sneer undergoes hyperbolic deviation and takes on a ludicrous dimension: the sneer features as dentures. Thus Uncle Bo's 'long yellow tusks like fangs' (*VD*, 79) surface in Anna's mind when a letter from Vincent Jeffries, Walter's cousin, tells her that Walter is breaking up with her. The letter is a turning-point in Anna's development as well as a crucial moment in the representation of the norm. Evaluation is carried out indirectly thanks to the full quotation of Vincent's letter and a time-shift referring us to the occasion when, as a child, Anna first saw her uncle's false teeth. This surprising analepsis[26] is a surrogate for narratorial comment. At first Anna fails to see the connection between the letter and her strange recollection. The connection has to be reconstructed, as it is the case for all ironies. The sneer, a trope for faceless malevolence, has now become a mere prosthesis, a trope for conventional cowardice (Walter Jeffries has not mustered up enough courage to tell Anna himself). The hyperbolic variant of the sneer no longer signifies cruelty or oppression, but pathetic sham. The decay of the elderly man's body, featuring in the text as a disconnected analepsis which the heroine herself cannot account for, is but a reflection of a disintegrating 'body politic' that has ceased to signify.

Good Morning Midnight also questions the legitimacy of patriarchal authority, revealing the various malfunctions of the social body and the meaningless codes shared by its members. This questioning is most apparent in the recollected scene in which Mr Blank, the boss of a fashion shop where Sasha used to work, pays his quarterly visit to his staff. Mr Blank interviews Sasha who, panic-stricken, loses her bearings. If her mind goes blank, Mr Blank is the butt of ironic evaluation. The episode shows that order, hierarchy, here embodied by this figure of economic power, is meaningless and can only generate chaos. Cross-examined about her qualifications for the position, Sasha cannot reveal the 'unspeakable' factors that got her the job but the reader is told thanks to her interior monologue: the manager's mistress kindly did a bit of string-pulling for her. Because society tolerates such practices as long as they are hushed up, Sasha is forced into meaningless tautology: 'I'm here because I'm here because I'm here' (*GMM*, 18). Order, then, through its aptly named representative, Mr Blank, is responsible for the failure of causality and for the heroine's disorientation, for even time and space are dismantled by Mr Blank's prescriptions. While Sasha finds it impossible to remember dates – 'years, days, hours, everything is a blank in my head' (*GMM*, 18) – the fashion shop becomes a maze. Sasha is supposed to take a letter 'to the kise' (*GMM*, 22), which is Mr Blank's mispronunciation of the French word '*caisse*'. Unable to understand what he means, she starts on a mad quest for meaning that will only entail a nightmarish dissolution of space. Mr Blank produces a blank signifier inducing the collapse of signifying structures and, symptomatically, when Sasha is summoned to his office, articulate speech goes missing. Having the feeling, for some reason, that Mr Blank wants to check up on her knowledge of foreign languages, she tries to remember the little German she knows and all she can think of is a nonsensical series of disconnected, incomplete sentences that, of course, make no sense at all (*GMM*, 21). She comes up with a bric-à-brac made of linguistic odds and ends, with repetition and parataxis as symptoms of the failure of organized thinking. The only logical sequence in this bric-à-brac is provided by the seven notes of the scale, in other words by something that stands outside articulate signification. The passage, however, derives some coherence from its overall tonality: Sasha's utterances consistently deal with loss, pain and cruelty. Meaning still operates on an implicit level while it no longer operates in the world ruled by Mr Blank. Again, the contrast between unspoken consistency and outspoken chaos is a token of the narrator's tongue-in-cheek.

Other symbols of authority and representatives of consensual codes are the butt of Jean Rhys's irony, among which is the judicial system, the most prescriptive institution of all. The judicial system produces a denotative discourse: its utterances can be declared right or wrong and put to the test of evidence, their legitimacy resting on univocality. Jean Rhys's texts constantly question – and so does irony – the validity of such normative univocality. Dealings with the law are one of the recurring motifs in her fiction, peopled with countless judges, lawyers, policemen, warders, and so on. The plot of *Quartet*, for instance, is framed by the arrest of Marya's husband and the end of his time in jail. Quite a few stories stage arrests, scenes in police stations or in courthouses. 'From a French Prison'[27] is set in a prison visiting-room. In 'Tigers Are Better-Looking', two characters are arrested for disorderly conduct. In 'Let Them Call It Jazz', the heroine is taken to Holloway Prison. In 'The Lotus',[28] an eccentric woman poet, one of whose poems is entitled 'The Convict's Mother', is arrested for running around in the nude and 'Fishy Waters'[29] is entirely devoted to the trial of a certain Jimmy Longa. In all these texts, the representation of the judicial is fundamentally ironic, the ironic effect being engineered by hyperbole. The law is each time presented as a sort of superlative spectacle tacitly exposing its meaninglessness.

In *Quartet*, for example, the 'Palais de Justice' is described as a majestic monument:

> Shining gates, ascending flights of steps. *Liberté, Egalité, Fraternité* in golden letters; *Tribunal de Police* in black. As it were, a vision of heaven and the Judgement. (*Q*, 25)

This architectural manifestation of ideology is ironically sacramentalized by the imagery of verticality ('ascending flight of steps') and the solemn motto on its pediment, by which the seat of human justice means to acquire a near-metaphysical dimension. However, the modulating phrase 'as it were' reveals the narrator's critical stance as well as the gap that separates the courthouse from any absolute notion of a divine justice. The phrase also designates the 'Palais de Justice' as a failed allegory. 'As it were' prevents the reader from readily identifying the building with the ideas it is supposed to stand for. Thus, the superlative description of the holy of holies gives way to the tacit construction of what must be taken as an empty shell in pompous attire.

The other flag-bearers of the law are equally magnified and devalued at one and the same time. Where they are concerned, characterization often verges on grotesque caricature. In 'Let Them Call It Jazz', for instance, a policewoman's foot expands in an almost supernatural way:

> She wear sandals and thick stockings and I never see a foot so big or so bad. It look like it want to mash up the whole world. Then she come in after the foot, and her face not so pretty either. (*Tigers*, 55)

This hackneyed metaphor for overbearing power is ironically revisited, the trope for oppression assuming a clownish dimension. Likewise, in 'From a French Prison', a warder is compared to 'a bloated, hairy insect born of the darkness and of the dank smell', to 'some petty god' (*Tigers*, 146), and is finally allegorized in the same ironic way as the courthouse in *Quartet*: '[t]here he was, the representative of honesty, of the law, of the stern forces of Good that punishes Evil' (*Tigers*, 146). Of course this grand dispenser of justice has none of the nobility of a knight: he is a low-browed creature with a heavy build, eyeing girls in a concupiscent way. Figure is altogether incompatible with function, which makes the allegory an irrelevant one.

This tendency towards caricature posits the law as a theatrical performance failing to produce meaning. While judicial discourse is supposed to be reliable, resting upon the production of irrefutable proof and strict causality, *Quartet* foregrounds the malfunctions of judicial meaning, especially when Marya desperately tries to discover the motive for Stephan's arrest. Every half-hour, she asks the same question: 'Why?' Invariably the answer is 'No information' (*Q*, 23). The reconstruction of causality is impeached by the very system that is supposed to help reconstruct it. Marya will eventually get an answer, but before she does, she is to experience sheer chaos, going from office to office, walking down endless corridors as if in an absurd maze. The way in which the narrator describes the end of her frantic wanderings is reminiscent of absurdist literature:

> She thought of all the corridors and staircases which had led her to his dim, musty-smelling room and felt bewildered and giddy.
> Both the lawyers laughed heartily and one of them threw his head back to do it, opening his mouth widely and showing a long pink and white tongue and the beginnings of a palate. (*Q*, 26)

The dismantling of causality ('bewildered and giddy')
and grotesque distortion produced by the close-up on
the lawyer's 'long pink and white tongue' foster the
representation of meaninglessness, all the more so as the
mouth has in the process ceased to be the organ of
articulate speech, where univocal utterances might have
been expected.

If the law is somewhat aphasic in *Quartet*, it
paradoxically is what cancels the advent of the truth in
'Let Them Call It Jazz':

> I want to speak up and tell [the magistrate] how they
> steal all my savings, so when my landlord asks for
> month's rent I haven't got it to give. I want to tell him
> the woman next door provoke me since long time
> and call me bad names but she have a soft sugar voice
> and nobody hear – that's why I broke her window,
> but I'm ready to buy another after all. I want to say all
> I do is sing in that old garden, and I want to say this
> in decent quiet voice. But I hear myself talking loud
> and I see my hands wave in the air. Too besides it's
> no use, they won't believe me, so I don't finish. I stop,
> and I feel the tears on my face. 'Prove it'. That's all
> they will say. (*Tigers*, 57)

Selina does not deny that she has been making trouble;
she is simply trying to reconstruct the causal sequence
that brought her to the courtroom. It seems, however,
that the tyranny of proof ('prove it') is what makes the
truth shy away, inducing either silence or irrational
behaviour. Moreover, the verdict indicates that the
magistrate has simply overlooked motivation, siding
with the various witnesses who all testified to gratuitous
troublemaking. While Selina pleads her cause in both
senses of the word, the law obliterates it.

In 'Fishy Waters', the magistrate's attitude is radically different. Judge Somers is wary of hearsay and does his utmost to dig out the truth. The trial of Jimmy Longa, who is charged with assault on a little girl, is nonetheless a deadlock. The sentence cannot be passed, Judge Somers being incapable of establishing the truth. This judicial aphasia can partly be ascribed to the historical context. The story is set in the 1890s in Dominica, fifty years after the end of slavery. Two racial communities, the Whites and the Blacks, are still antagonistic to each other. There is no consensus in the island's divided society and the courthouse cannot count on consensus to issue a clear verdict, as it does in 'Let Them Call It Jazz', for instance. In fact Jimmy Longa is the not too sound basis for a frail consensus that momentarily deflects the focus away from mutual hatred. White and black communities band together against the figure of Jimmy Longa, a *pharmakos* or 'scape-goat' (*Sleep*, 46). He is a foreign body among the colonials on account of his working-class background and of his socialist ideas. His behaviour is deemed highly improper by the Whites: he is a drunkard and settles in a black neighbourhood, which is not done. As Maggie Penrice puts it in her letter, he becomes 'an honorary Black' in the white community (*Sleep*, 48). On the other hand, as a white outcast stripped of any form of power that might have held open antagonism in check, Jimmy Longa also falls prey to black harassment. The magistrate is clever enough not to mistake this witch-hunt for direct evidence and clearly spells out the failure of the hermeneutic quest:

> I am not here to speculate and I cannot accept either hearsay evidence or innuendoes supported by no evidence; but I have not been in my post for twenty years without learning that it is extremely difficult to obtain direct evidence here. (*Sleep*, 58–9)

The fragmented structure of the story reflects this failed quest for the truth as well as the prominence of the hearsay mode. 'Fishy Waters' is a multi-levelled narrative, made up of several texts pieced together. In the first few pages, it reproduces a series of letters to the editor of the local newspaper, *The Dominica Herald*, then a letter from Maggie Penrice, wife to the main witness for the prosecution, to Caroline, a friend of hers, which all deal with the case. The story then moves on to a paraphrase, including extensive quotations, of the news coverage of the case, which itself draws upon the minutes of the trial. Only in the last three pages does the narrative go back to the diegetic level, namely the aftermath of the trial. Thus, narrating voices proliferate, putting up a number of discursive screens between the reader and the event. The trial or the alleged attack themselves are never staged directly, while Jimmy Longa, who does not show up in the courthouse, is nowhere to be seen. To cap it all, the victim suffers from amnesia. Thus the story rests upon a number of absentees, Jimmy Longa, the attack, the trial, and finally the ever-receding truth, which lies somewhere '*sub judice*' (*Sleep*, 47).

In the final analysis, the story tends to show that the most prescriptive of discourses, the judicial one, fails to articulate the truth. In Jean Rhys's ironic representation of the law, judicial discourse is either equated with rumour, the group's voice, regardless of hard facts ('Let Them Call It Jazz'), or defeated by hearsay ('Fishy Waters'). Irony or the rhetoric of the unspoken unsettles the dominant idiom by positing the truth as the unspeakable other, thus conferring upon masculine discourse the status of a lie.

5 *Voyage in the Dark*: 'Two Tunes'

If the figures of the law are systematically debunked, so is another set of rules, language itself. *Voyage in the Dark* and *Good Morning Midnight*, each in a different way, build a code of feminine resistance to linguistic authority which simultaneously probes into the locus of the feminine. Both seem to define the feminine as a subversive force waging war against the master discourse. Jean Rhys develops an ethics of subversion akin to that which underlies Kristeva's linguistic theory: for Julia Kristeva, the feminine can simply be defined as 'that which cannot be represented, what is not said, what remains above and beyond nomenclatures and ideologies'.[1] According to her, femininity, regardless of biological categories, is but one form of marginality among many and can be analysed as any other struggle against a centralized power structure. From the margin, then, Jean Rhys develops signifying structures other than those provided by consensual discourse which, as we have seen, tend to obliterate the truth.

In *Voyage in the Dark*, this subversive quest for an alternative is carried out through a binary opposition between two spaces, the idyllic West Indian island the eighteen-year-old heroine comes from and England, the grim motherland where she has come to seek her fortune. This opposition is rendered through the correlation of two narrative levels: while the diegesis is set in England, constant reference is made to Anna's home island in the shape of remembrances or of a mental, silent subtext whose ceaseless surfacing seems to exert

pressure on the diegetic text. In this unspoken yet
written subtext prevails a signifying mode that is
reminiscent of what Julia Kristeva calls the *chora*. The
chora is the shifting, indeterminate receptacle of pre-
Oedipal drives that 'precedes and underlies figuration
and thus specularization, and is analogous only to vocal
or kinetic rhythm'.[2] The semiotic *chora* is the first pre-
verbal signifying mode before entry into the Symbolic
Order; it is 'a modality of signifiance in which the
linguistic sign is not yet articulated as the absence of an
object and as the distinction between real and symbolic'.[3] It is then part of the formation of the signifying
process (*procès de signifiance*) which Julia Kristeva defines
as the interaction between the semiotic and the symbolic.
Once the subject has entered into the Symbolic Order,
the *chora* is more or less successfully repressed and
might surface as pulsional pressure on symbolic language, 'only in *dream* logic, however, [...] or in certain
signifying practices, such as the text',[4] where it can be
perceived 'as contradictions, meaninglessness, disruption, silences and absences in the symbolic language'.[5]
Thus, the *chora* is a pre-verbal, rhythmic ordering rather
than a new language. It constitutes, in other words, 'the
heterogeneous, disruptive dimension of language, that
which can never be caught up in the closure of
traditional linguistic theory'.[6]

The West Indian *Chora*

It is undeniable that, as Deborah Kloepfer argues, 'Jean
Rhys's fiction operates around an economy of loss – loss
of language, loss of homeland, loss of economic and
sexual power, and loss of the mother.'[7] This is even
truer of *Voyage in the Dark*, in which Anna, setting foot in
England, loses just about everything she ever possessed,

including her virginity. More than ever, if one refers to the main line of the narrative, Anna Morgan seems to be limited to the identity of a sexual *object*: she is a virgin gradually becoming a prostitute. This journey into deprivation and destitution is, however, counteracted by the narrative strategy of the novel. For the first time in her novelistic practice, Jean Rhys makes use of the first-person narrative – a narrative mode she will, from *Voyage in the Dark* on, remain faithful to – by which Anna, the heroine–narrator, seems to be promoted to the status of the speaking *subject*. Loss is indeed compensated for by the production of a text, Anna's own text, and absence, the obsessional issue in Anna's diegetic existence, is converted into textual presence through Anna's own authorship.

According to Nancy R. Harrison,

Rhys's writing presents a continuing dialogue with the dominant language, and at the same time makes explicit the place of a woman's own language. This place is one Rhys makes out of the stuff of the other language, within the context of which she is forced to live as well as to speak. In writing, the speaking of the language is transformed. Rhys *writes* what her characters may not, do not, *say out loud*.[8]

This dialogic structure, which Nancy R. Harrison makes out to be the trademark of women's writing, may be seen as the object of inquiry in *Voyage in the Dark*, a bias made even clearer by its original title, *Two Tunes*.[9] The 'two tunes' inform the structure of the novel in which two narrative levels are intertwined, the level of what the character does not 'say out loud' speaking back to the first narrative, the locus of Englishness, or ethnocentric and phallocentric dominance. In one of her letters, Jean Rhys describes her project in the following terms: '[t]he

big idea – well I'm blowed if I can be sure what it is.
Something to do with time being an illusion I think.
I mean that the past exists side by side with the present,
not behind it; that what was – is.'[10] In *Voyage in the Dark*,
the unspoken makes up as much as half of the text: no
less than fourteen evocations of Anna's extradiegetic
past come to resurrect her native island, not to mention
the last part of the novel, where the West Indies are
blended into England in a bout of delirium subsequent
to Anna's abortion. One of her conversations with
Walter Jeffries (*VD*, 44–9) is emblematic of the paradoxically overbearing presence of the lost island in
Anna's text: first, the topic of their dialogue is the history
of Anna's family, her uncle Ramsay, her slave-owning
ancestors, and so on; in addition, Anna's spoken lines
are interspersed with silent ones, again dealing with her
island, which are fitted into the actualized conversation
thanks to the silent soliloquy that invariably accompanies
any dialogue. Anna's island then acquires considerable
textual presence, a presence rooted in the reality of
geographical space, for Anna's countless references to it
are supplemented by a quotation from a travel book
indicating the precise position on the globe of that
distant, yet retrievable space (*VD*, 15).

Not only is loss compensated for by the written text
but the island stands as an alternative to life in England.
It is depicted as an idyllic world, a kind of Arcadia where
the individual communes with nature. On many occasions, it reads as the locus of *jouissance*, that is, 'the direct
reexperience of the physical pleasures of infancy and of
later sexuality, repressed but not obliterated by the Law
of the Father'.[11] It seems that this *jouissance* has survived
cultural pressures towards sublimation to surface in
Anna's private subtext. Until the episode in which Anna
tells us of her first menstruation, which, as we shall see,
corresponds to the end of the golden age in Anna's life,

the island can be seen as the seat of semiotic continuum, the alternative signifying mode operating from bodily experience and the pleasures derived from it. The prevalence of the senses in Anna's island appears as early as in the first passage devoted to it, in which Anna enumerates the great variety of smells, up to twelve different ones, still wafting in her memory:

> Market Street smelt of the wind, but the narrow street smelt of niggers and wood-smoke and salt fishcakes fried in lard. [...] It was funny, but that was what I thought about more than anything else – the smell of the streets and the smells of frangipanni and lime juice and cinnamon and cloves. (*VD*, 7)

After the first descriptive sentence, the syntax seems to mimic the fulfilling immediacy of Anna's relationship with the world, the omission of the verb and the repetition of 'and' conveying the synchronic fullness of experience, its instantaneousness. The world appeals to the senses and reality is endowed with extraordinary materiality or body. It is dense, carnal, and the colours, for instance, are more vivid than in England (*VD*, 47). Francine, Anna's black alter ego, epitomizes this jubilant blending with the world through the senses. In one of the analepses, she can be seen digging her teeth into a mango with unsuppressed pleasure and in such a way as to ensure optimal fulfilment:

> Her teeth would bite into the mango and her lips fasten on either side of it, and while she sucked you saw that she was perfectly happy. When she had finished she always smacked her lips twice, very loud – louder than you could believe possible. It was a ritual. (*VD*, 58)

The close-up on each of her ritual moves, rendered as if in slow motion, underlines the fullness of the moment. Through the foregrounding of the senses, of a fulfilling bodily experience, Jean Rhys expresses nostalgia for a pre-verbal contact with the world, a pre-referential clinch or continuum prior to symbolic splitting.

This economy of fulfilment gives rise to an alternative mode of communication, an ideal or semiotic code shared by Anna and Francine, preserving continuity. Symptomatically, Hester, Anna's stepmother and main representative of English culture in the context of Anna's childhood, makes no sense of it:

> She [Hester] always hated Francine.
> 'What do you talk about?' she used to say.
> 'We don't talk about anything', I'd say. 'We just talk'.
> But she didn't believe me. (*VD*, 58)

Hester's query bears on the object of the little girls' exchanges; in her eyes, one necessarily talks *about* something. She subscribes to the traditional conception of the sign as a substitute for the extra-linguistic, as the absence of an object, as resulting from the symbolic break. No wonder she cannot relate to the girls' discourse which is rooted in a signifying logic that is other, in which speaking – as opposed to speaking about something – affords perfect communication and con-jures up reality as if by magic. Arcadian speech is an all-encompassing, hyper-performative speech act bridging the splits between signifier and signified, sign and referent. In Anna's childhood haven, the sign system the two girls share is not synonymous with absence and separation but partakes of presence and continuity.

This ideal sign that bypasses the symbolic split is of course chimerical: indeed, the text does not articulate it, leaving the content of the girls' conversations, as well as the stories that Francine tells Anna, unwritten. Here, however, Jean Rhys celebrates a language that is not divorced from reality, a language which seems to be derived from the laws of nature rather than the law of the father. The episode of Anna's first menstruation reveals how extraordinarily in tune with the natural rhythms of the body Francine's words are. Francine makes Anna feel as if 'it was all in the day's work like eating or drinking', but Hester steps in, 'her eyes wandering all over the place', and Anna chokes and wants to die (*VD*, 59). After Hester's intrusion, the natural order is forever disrupted and culture rushes in to dispense a series of inhibitions and prohibitions that alienate Anna from her body, from now on associated with a set of prescriptions. This onslaught of symbolic meaning on semiotic continuity coincides with the end of Anna's Arcadian life, with the moment when she is expelled from her childhood Eden.

It therefore coincides with Anna's entry into the symbolic order and the time of history, which are contiguous according to Julia Kristeva:

> The symbolic order – the order of verbal communication, the paternal order of genealogy – is a temporal order. For the speaking animal, it is the clock of objective time: it provides the reference point, and, consequently, all possibilities of measurement, by distinguishing between a before, a now and an after.[12]

Before the invasion of culture through the operation of Hester, the island's temporality seems to be immune to linear time, the time of history, which is also that of speech considered as the enunciation of a *sequence* of words. Francine, for instance, is ageless and seems to hold the secret of eternal youth: 'if you wash your face in fresh coconut-water every day you are always young and unwrinkled, however long you live' (*VD*, 129).

Moreover, the ritual way in which she tells her stories is based on repetitive rhythms rather than narrative linearity: '[s]ometimes she told me stories, and at the start of the story she had to say "Timm, timm", and I had to answer "Bois sèche"' (*VD*, 61). When it comes to Francine's storytelling, the text does not reproduce a sequence of events but the preliminary unchanging formulae – typical of oral tradition in the West Indies – that signal passage into another signifying mode, in which there is no before, no now and no after, no cleavage between matrix and copy, between the sign and reality. Arcadia, then, is not subject to linearity, separation or decline through time. Its temporality is cyclical and eternal – as, Julia Kristeva argues, women's time is[13] – which is suggested by the tutelage of the moon. The islanders are wary of the sun and shy away from it, while 'moonlight rows' (*VD*, 46) or moonlight picnics (*VD*, 139) are much favoured. They tend to cut themselves off from solar time, giving themselves up instead to the influence of the moon, to the eternal recurrence of its cycles that secure eternal renewal.

This cyclical, lunar time, however, is easily disrupted. When Hester takes it upon herself to explain to Anna the various rules pertaining to her new womanhood in the passage quoted earlier, she puts an end to a temporality in which the perennial repetition of a biological rhythm simply conforms to the rhythms of nature. She reintroduces socio-symbolic clockwork characterized by linear chronology: triggers off, in short, the time of history which Anna sees as the time of the Whites:

> Being white and getting like Hester, and all the things you get – old and sad and everything. I kept thinking, 'No ... No ... No ...' And I knew that day that I'd started to grow old and nothing could stop it. (*VD*, 62)

All of a sudden, Anna is precipitated into solar time, the temporality of the dominant order, a plunge which the text materializes in the systematic scansion of time-markers and in a minutely detailed account of all that happened on that day (*VD*, 59–63). As a metaphor for her subjection to symbolic temporality, Anna, determined to die, stays out in the sun in the hottest hours of the day until it hurts and she gets sick (*VD*, 63). Here Anna painfully steps into history, adulthood and white-hood all at once. This is the point where she really loses her semiotic virginity, as the imagery of castration – 'The pain was like knives' (*VD*, 63) – leads us to think. This is, Coral Ann Howells comments, 'the beginning of Anna's gendered narrative'.[14]

England, or the Imperialistic Sign

It is not until her arrival in England, however, that her loss of virginity will become effective. Leaving the virgin island of her childhood for good, Anna lands in the realm of culture in which codes or encoded reality, as opposed to the island's immediate, raw reality, are given pride of place. In England, the sign is not only a substitute for absence, in accordance with its traditional function, but it tends to be the only reality. London, the imperial metropolis, is the seat of an imperialistic sign system which, far from simply standing for the extra-linguistic, tends to annihilate it. A walk around the neighbourhood of Primrose Hill on a rainy day is enough, for instance, to make Anna feel that 'there's not anything else anywhere, that it's all made up that there is anything else' (*VD*, 78). London, it seems, has absorbed the rest of the world, in much the same way as the sign acquires the status of an engulfing totality. Thus, after the Arcadian sign system that she used to

share with Francine, Anna is faced with a new category
of signs which no longer refer to extra-linguistic reality
but to more signs, more codes. The opening image of
the curtain that comes to blot everything out on Anna's
arrival in England – 'It was as if a curtain had fallen,
hiding everything I had ever known. It was almost like
being born again' (*VD*, 7) – bears witness to this fore-
closure of reality.

Generally speaking, codes are foregrounded in
England: people, for instance, pay obsessive attention
to codes of dress and behaviour. To be acquainted with
and to conform to them is a bare necessity. Those who
are not 'beautifully dressed' (*VD*, 22) come up against
sneering contempt. While corporeal reality was a
component part of the world in Arcadia, it is hidden,
insulated and subordinated to encoded appearances in
England. Part of the representation of symbolic supremacy is the text's emphasis on cultural artefacts. Everywhere, prints exhibit the models prized by British
society. In Ethel Matthews's flat, for instance, the
furnishings, the chintz cushions and the reproductions
of the *Cries of London* are contrived so as to build up the
image of respectability to which Ethel, a '*masseuse*', has a
claim (*VD*, 119). A respectable appearance, painstakingly
elaborated in accordance with the code of respectability,
is all that counts. Another print in Anna's bedroom
celebrates loyalty – 'over the bed the picture of the dog
sitting up begging – *Loyal Heart*' (*VD*, 127) – while the
hotel in Savernake where Anna spends a few days with
Walter Jeffries is simply packed with such ideological
role-models, namely prints titled 'The Sailor's Farewell',
'The Sailor's Return', 'Reading the Will' or 'Conjugal
Affection' (*VD*, 66). These prints are by no means
mimetic: they do not reflect reality so much as the text
of tradition. As Victorian allegories, they seek to
promote a number of values, with the support of

normative captions contributing to the creation of some ideal order which is being handed down to the younger generation. That the prints do not reflect reality is made clear by the fact that, each time, the diegetic situations stand in contrapuntal relation to the message delivered by the print. Ethel is not respectable – she runs a massage parlour; loyalty is simply unheard of in her world – she dismisses Anna when she learns that she is pregnant – and women, not dogs, are cast in the role of beggars. Similarly, the tense atmosphere in Savernake is far removed from any notion of 'conjugal affection' or domestic happiness, and sailors do not return: the outing to Savernake turns out to be a farewell party and Anna's affair with Walter virtually comes to an end there. The prevalence of the code, conveyed through the use of prints, can also be observed in one of the stories, 'Till September Petronella'. There, again, the print does not come second to reality (it is not mimetic); it seems to generate it. The farmer who takes Petronella back to London claims that he knows what women want:

> They like a bit of loving, that's what they like, isn't it? A bit of loving. All women like that. [...] And they like pretty dresses and bottles of scent, and bracelets with blue stones in them. (*Tigers*, 26)

The context suggests that his somewhat stereotyped vision of women is by no means derived from first-hand experience of flesh-and-blood women but from a painting of Lady Hamilton that he has been staring at while droning out his clichés. The painting, like the prints in *Voyage in the Dark*, is not so much a copy as a matrix: it generates reality and prescribes behaviour. This usurping of the matrix function prompts Anna to become an angry iconoclast. One evening, after a few drinks, she shatters to pieces the picture of 'Loyal Heart'

(*VD*, 137), a symbol of her own abasement, in what can be seen as a desperate attempt to challenge the antecedent position of the cultural artefact and the sense of inevitability that derives from it.

Books equally seem to generate reality. Where England is concerned, books come first and reality second: 'I had read about England ever since I could read – smaller meaner everything is never mind –' (*VD*, 15). Not only does reality come second but it also comes as a major disappointment to the female colonial who has had no direct experience of the imperial metropolis. Of course, this mediated knowledge of England pertains to the colonial's outlook, the antecedence of the book also reflecting the way in which a strange culture has been imposed upon him or her. On the other hand, Anna's statement highlights the general supremacy of the sign in the metropolis, a supremacy that bestows upon the extra-linguistic a subsidiary position. More importantly, Anna herself is generated by a printed model, Zola's Nana. She is, as Coral Ann Howells puts it, 'already en-gendered/en-cultured'.[15] When Anna first appears in the diegesis, she is reading *Nana*, a book 'about a tart' (*VD*, 9), the analogy between the two heroines being underlined by the anagrammatic relationship of their names. As Anna gradually drifts into prostitution, her destiny indeed becomes more and more like Nana's, but the striking thing is that Anna proceeds from Nana, from a printed script that itself reproduces one of the few cultural scripts available to women. Here it is to be noted that Anna's itinerary greatly differs from that of Marya in *Quartet*: Marya was gradually made to conform to a script elaborated by the Heidlers, while Anna is altogether generated by a set pattern in a world where codes and signs generate experience. What Anna experiences with Walter, her first lover, is already written in the great book of culture, as people keep reminding her: '[e]verybody says the man's bound to get tired and you read it in all books. But I never read now, so they can't get at me like that, anyway' (*VD*, 64). Anna might have given up reading, but the script is there for everybody to read. Again, cultural artefacts will everywhere prophesy what she is meant to become: in one of the rooms she moves into, little china ornaments displayed on the mantelshelf include 'a geisha with a kimono and sash in colours and a little naked woman lying on her stomach with a feather in her hair' (*VD*, 90). There is no deviating from the generative script. Anna's necessary compliance with this preordained pattern of life is represented in a passage where she quotes from one of her landladies' once unfair expostulation: '"[c]rawling up the stairs at three o'clock in the morning. [. . .] I don't want no tarts in my house, so now you know"' (*VD*, 26). At the time, innocent Anna had done nothing to substantiate her landlady's innuendoes. Some time later, however, she does indeed sneak up to her room with Walter Jeffries in the small hours:

> '*Crawling up the stairs at three o'clock in the morning*', she said. *Well, I'm crawling up the stairs.*
>   I stopped. I wanted to say, 'No, I've changed my mind'. But he laughed and squeezed my hand and said, 'What's the matter? Come on, be brave'. (*VD*, 32)

The repetition of the landlady's words, as well as Anna's feeble resistance to Walter's encouragements convey the inexorability of the script.

Symmetrically, as the sign proliferates and expands, the extra-linguistic withers or thins out in the English 'tune'. *Voyage in the Dark* is riddled with metaphors of a mortified reality which stands in sharp contrast with the lush natural world of Anna's virgin island. When Anna

first sees England, for instance, she discovers a skimpy,
partitioned landscape, 'divided into squares like pocket-
handkerchiefs; a small tidy look it had everywhere
fenced off from everywhere else' (*VD*, 15). In Southsea,
the down-market seaside resort where she meets Walter,
the garden is 'walled-in' and the tree 'by the back wall
was lopped so that it looked like a man with stumps
instead of arms and legs' (*VD*, 9). In London, 'the air is
used-up and dead, dirty-warm, as if thousands of other
people had breathed it before you' (*VD*, 65). The
natural, non-encoded world is dying out in England,
like the Caribs whom Anna refers to after the end of her
affair with Walter. Under the pressure of the imperialistic sign, at the hands of European colonizers, the
Caribs have become practically extinct:

> 'The Caribs indigenous to this island were a warlike
> tribe and their resistance to white domination,
> though spasmodic, was fierce. [...] They are now
> practically exterminated. The few hundreds that are
> left do not intermarry with the Negroes. Their
> reservation, at the northern end of the island, is
> known as the Carib Quarter'. (*VD*, 91)

The Caribs, a metaphor for the near-extinct virgin
origin, are subjected to the same partitioning as the
English landscape, Anna drawing an analogy between
discursive and political imperialisms. This conflation of
imperialisms is represented by the fact that here Anna is
quoting from a book: her text can only refer to another
text; the 'real' Caribs are 'practically exterminated' and
have been colonized by discourse. Imperialism has
produced reservations and discursive proliferation at
the expense of indigenous, colonized reality.

On the face of it, Anna, like the Caribs, succumbs
to the imperialistic sign system with which she clashes,

mostly in England. After a few months there, her language has become divorced from reality, as she notices herself:

> when I began to talk about the flowers out there I got that feeling of a dream, of two things that I couldn't fit together, and it was as if I were making up the names. Stephanotis, hibiscus, yellow-bell, jasmine, frangipanni, corolita. (*VD*, 67)

This endless round of signifiers, disconnected from their signifieds and referents, is not only emblematic of the symbolic split that now affects Anna's once semiotic language; it also spells out the triumph of a self-sufficient sign that no longer stands for reality ('the flowers out there' have no more substance than a dream). Like the Caribs, Anna has been colonized by the dominant order which now infuses her language. Similarly, her life has conformed to the various codes designed to generate it. By gradually slipping into prostitution, she lives out the narrative society prescribes, and ends up parroting prior textualizations, among which is *Nana*. Her almost bleeding to death after her abortion may be seen as a metaphor for the exhaustion arising from symbolic imperialism. Anna's 'voyage', it seems, has led her nowhere but to this wan condition, which is suggested by the title of the novel: the preposition 'in', where 'into' might have been expected, emphasizes the fact that she can only remain in the same space. By moving to England, Anna has entered the deadlock of a hyper-symbolic island, an intransitive sign system offering no escape route, in which signs and people alike go round in circles, 'in the dark'. At the end of the novel, she rightly sees her future as grim repetition, even though her last words may sound hopeful:

When their voices stopped the ray of light came in
again under the door like the last thrust of remembering before everything is blotted out. I lay and watched
it and thought about starting all over again. And about
being new and fresh. And about mornings, and misty
days, when anything might happen. And about
starting all over again, all over again ... (*VD*, 159)

This is a revised ending into which Jean Rhys was
requested to introduce a more cheerful note by her
publishers – Anna dies in the original ending; but
Anna's prospects could look brighter. The above
passage bears witness to an inevitable repetitive pattern,
leaving little doubt as to the nature of Anna's 'fresh
start'. One can argue, however, that Anna's defeat is not
complete, for her 'tune' rings on and permeates the
dominant one in the last part of the novel.

Utopia

Becoming aware that her life is at odds with her desires
and that she is unable to reconcile them within the
prison-house of the phallogocentric order into which
she has been precipitated, Anna, nevertheless, does not
resign herself to silence. Even as she comes to the
realization that the Arcadian world of her childhood is
irretrievably lost, she manages to resurrect Arcadia and
its alternative signifying mode in what can be described
as a utopian text. Far from being repressed, her desires
find a way into language, articulating a text congruent
with Anna's longing for continuity.

The conversion of 'Paradise lost' into a utopian space
starts towards the end of Part Three, with a dream in
which Anna, sailing 'in a dolls' sea transparent as glass',
finds herself unable to land on her miniature island:

And the ship was sailing very close to an island, which
was home except that the trees were all wrong. These
were English trees, their leaves trailing in the water.
I tried to catch hold of a branch and step ashore, but
the deck of the ship expanded. (*VD*, 140)

The dream provides a clear reflection of the imperialism
of the English sign: the tropical space is typically
pervaded by 'English trees', absorbed by the imperial
metropolis, an absorption also conveyed by the belittle-
ment of the Caribbean islands – 'dolls of islands'
(*VD*, 140) – and the reification of a sea turned solid.
The supernatural expansion(ism) of the ship's deck
lends further weight to the representation of imperialism, but it also denies access to the West Indian reality,
thus pointing to the advent of utopia. Indeed, in this
text which constantly moves back and forth between past
and present, hardly any reference is made to Anna's
native island between this point and the beginning of
Anna's fit of delirium, as if it had been crushed out of
existence, struck off the map – there is in fact but one
short reference to it (*VD*, 151). This can be read as a tacit
acknowledgement on Anna's part that there is no space
in language or in cultural practice for what she desires.
As a result, the island ceases to function as a referential
absentee Anna longs to retrieve, and becomes instead a
non-space, a utopia which, by definition, is a self-
referential, purely textual construct.

This utopian construction prevails in the last pages of
Voyage in the Dark (*VD*, 156–8), where the narrative of
Anna's slow descent into prostitution gives way to
interior monologue as she lies in her bed, only half-
conscious, after her abortion. On the borderline
between life and death, consciousness and unconscious-
ness, she seems to be able to articulate an aesthetic of
continuity akin to the semiotic economy of her Arcadian

childhood, regardless of the script into which she has
been forced. The italicized monologue abruptly plunges
the reader into the middle of an ongoing thought
process, in which West Indian and English scenes are
blended, as they are in Anna's dream: the monologue
starts with a reference to Masquerade, moves on to the
evocation of what we understand is a ball, then leaps on
to two different episodes in England and finally to one
of the most enigmatic passages in the novel, a horse ride
to Constance Estate when Anna was twelve. A few
unitalicized words providing a transition back to the
diegetic level interrupt Anna's silent soliloquy – ' "It
ought to be stopped", Mrs Polo said. "I'm giddy", I said.
"I'm awfully giddy" ' (*VD*, 157) – but, although the
typography makes it clear that there is an alteration of
narrative level and that these words are not part of
Anna's rambling thoughts, they are immediately incorporated into the monologue's flux, which annihilates the
typographical attempt at clarification. Thus Anna's
utopian text undermines all boundaries, abolishing
time, space and traditional structures of meaning. On
several occasions, for example, identity is challenged by
a confusion of pronouns, making it difficult for the
reader to determine to whom they refer.[16] By the end of
the book, the 'two tunes' are no longer separate: all
narrative levels are merged in the magma of Anna's
stream of consciousness. Time present and times past
interweave and interact, while her mostly unpunctuated
sentences ostentatiously unsettle syntactic laws and
separations to give rise to an undifferentiated continuum borne along by associative memory, each thought
or memory triggering the next.

One of the most significant elements in this monologue is the remembered Masquerade that surfaces in
Anna's mind among other memories. Such a reference
at this point of the narrative is of course no accident. Not

so much a motif as an organizing principle, it partakes of
the subversive quality of Anna's text and points to its
carnivalesque nature. According to Mikhail Bakhtin,[17]
carnival is a popular, anti-authoritarian tradition, challenging official law and culture. The carnivalesque
aesthetic celebrates the anarchic, body-based and grotesque elements of popular culture in an attempt to
discrown the powers that be. Carnival, however, is not a
merely negative, oppositional process. As well as being
disruptive and irreverent, it is also a joyful affirmation of
regeneration and renewal. Thus, carnival is a fundamentally ambivalent ritual which simultaneously negates
and affirms, inverts hierarchies, undermines boundaries, brings together life and death, the elevated and
the low, with a view to asserting the material and bodily
continuity of human life. Momentarily suspending the
laws and restrictions of normal life, carnival is a time
outside time, a utopian space where contraries may
coexist, where the gay relativity of all things is
proclaimed. Within the context of Jean Rhys's novel,
the West Indian Masquerade is of course not so positive
as carnival in early modern Europe – Mikhail Bakhtin
focuses on the latter. There is evidence that the three
days of the Masquerade is an occasion for deep-seated
racial antagonisms to come to a head: while the Blacks
parade dressed up as grotesque Whites, sticking their
tongues out at them, the Whites, apprehensive and
acutely aware of the underlying violence of the
Masquerade, disapprovingly watch it from inside their
houses – '*it ought to be stopped somebody said it's not a decent
and respectable way to go on it ought to be stopped*' (*VD*, 156).
Far from abolishing distance between men and in spite
of the carnivalesque status reversal, the unruly Masquerade builds up a wall between the two communities.
As a white child, Anna does not participate in it but she
nonetheless seems to commune with eccentric carnival

laughter: '*I knew why the masks were laughing*' (*VD*, 157).
If, on the face of it, carnival is but a spectacle for her,
hers is more than a passive role. What she could not
achieve then (participation in the abolition of boundaries), she achieves in her monologue, issuing a
carnivalized text, a verbal masquerade which reproduces, within its own structures and by its own practice,
the characteristic discrownings of carnival proper, in
order to make way for a new logic exceeding that of
codified discourse.

The carnivalesque logic of her text consists, as we have
seen, in abolishing boundaries: Anna merges narrative levels (the two 'tunes' are one and the same) or
infringes syntactic laws (traditional marks of punctuation
are deleted and at times replaced by dashes). Conventional logical hinges are further challenged by non-
exclusive opposition: the whole of Part Four knits
together images of life and death, lushness and aridity,
fecundity and sterility. A good example of this combination is the allusion to the road to Constance Estate,
which is referred to for the second time in the novel at
the end of the italicized text. Intermingled with colour-
ful images of carnivalesque festivities, the reference to
the ride up to the family's estate leads to a barren world:

> – *a cold moon looking down on a place where nobody is a*
> *place full of stones where nobody is* (*VD*, 158)

Once the symbol of Arcadian cyclical regeneration, the
moon now presides over a deserted wasteland. This
ambivalent symbol is emblematic of a text that has its
roots in carnivalesque ambivalence which, again, can be
traced in the situation itself: while Anna has just had an
abortion, she gives birth to a regenerated discourse. If
the haemorrhage that is responsible for her giddiness

and mental confusion drains her body of life, her bleeding seems to be, simultaneously, what allows for the emergence of this carnivalesque text. Thus Anna's diegetic journey towards this exhausted, fruitless condition is itself the yeast for discursive renewal. This could be seen as Jean Rhys's own modernized reading of the grotesque body theorized by Mikhail Bakhtin, a body of becoming, process and change. Anna's bleeding, secreting, open body is reminiscent of the way in which Mikhail Bakhtin describes the Kerch terracotta figurines of senile, pregnant hags:

> This is typical and very strongly expressed grotesque. It is pregnant death, a death that gives birth. There is nothing completed, nothing calm and stable in the bodies of these old hags. They combine senile, decaying, and deformed flesh with the flesh of new life, conceived but yet unformed.[18]

Anna's body presents the same ambivalent combination of life and death, and one could sum up this paradoxical fecundity through another (carnivalesque) reversal: the body as sign is converted into a sign producer. What lies bloodless is not so much a body in its material corporeality as a cultural construct: Anna has become a prostitute in accordance with the script she was, from the start, meant to fit into. In the final monologue, Anna declares the death of this printed body and gives birth to a utopian, undifferentiated text transgressing conventional separations and categories and implicitly undermining those active in the identification of gender roles.

6 *Good Morning Midnight*: 'Every Word I Say Has Chains Round its Ankles'

In *Good Morning Midnight*, Jean Rhys's fourth novel published in 1939, dissent is manifested in a different way. While Anna in *Voyage in the Dark* tried to assert the existence of an alternative signifying mode, Sasha Jansen, a more experienced heroine, chooses controlled, parodic mimicry of the master discourse. Mimicking the mimicry imposed upon woman, she tries to undo the effects of patriarchal logic by overdoing them. Sasha is a middle-aged woman returning to Paris for a short holiday. She too is an outsider but, unlike the other heroines who go to great lengths to voice their difference, Sasha is intent on hiding it. One of the figures of this deliberate obliteration of difference is the novel's concern with intertextuality. This concept, coined by Julia Kristeva, refers to the ways in which any literary text is inseparably linked to other literary texts. Drawing upon Mikhail Bakhtin's theory of dialogism, Julia Kristeva argues that 'any text is constructed as a mosaic of quotations; any text is the absorption and transformation of another'.[1] She believes, along with other theorists, that intertextuality is the very condition of literature. Like any literary text, *Good Morning*

Midnight is woven from the tissues of other texts, but as well as being implicitly intertextual, it makes explicit use of intertextuality by overtly borrowing from a great variety of prior textual units, literary or non-literary, through direct citations or allusions. So great is the extent of these borrowings that *Good Morning Midnight* may be regarded as a dramatization of intertextuality. Its status as a self-conscious intertext is suggested by the title, a line from Poem 425 by Emily Dickinson, two stanzas of which serve as an epigraph. In the course of reading, one comes across other literary texts by Rimbaud, Keats, Racine and Oscar Wilde, to give but a few examples, while *Hamlet* or Molly Bloom's mono-logue in *Ulysses* are less directly alluded to. In addition to these references, the novel draws from a wide range of non-literary texts such as an operetta (*GMM*, 13), popular songs (*GMM*, 77), advice columns in women's magazines (*GMM*, 52–3), love letters (*GMM*, 73, 112), or even previous extradiegetic conversations, riddled with clichés and commonplaces. There is evidence, given the great number and diversity of the borrowed texts, that the main issue in the novel is not only this dialogical relation of any text to others but the relation of the text to, so to say, its raw material, language itself as a constraining, ready-made form, as a common stock of linguistic procedures and conventions. Indeed, Sasha tends to quote from rather than speak a language which is felt as a strange and coercive system from which the female speaking subject is alienated.

Good Morning Midnight is in fact a highly paradoxical novel as the Dickinsonian oxymoron that Jean Rhys chose for a title suggests. The paradox lies in the co-presence of this exacerbated intertextuality and of a narrative strategy which, in principle, should make for the idiosyncratic expression of the self. For the novel, written in the first person and in the present tense, is at

times close to interior monologue, so that the reader
may expect to become acquainted with the intricacies of
one particular self, with its most intimate thoughts,
through a spontaneous stream of consciousness. Autodiegetic narrative[2] or interior monologue necessarily
foreground the subject, whose voice, vision and psy-
chology originate the text. Although Sasha, as the
almighty centre of consciousness controlling the narrative, might have produced a highly integrated text, her
voice is constantly interfered with by heterogeneous
voices or discourses. I propose to explore this interference and its effects.

Who is Speaking?

Like *Voyage in the Dark*, *Good Morning Midnight* resorts to
autodiegetic narrating, but its narrative strategy differs
from that employed in *Voyage in the Dark*. *Voyage in the
Dark* is a retrospective, past-tense narrative in which the
distance between narrating 'I' and narrated 'I' remains
unresolved,[3] except in a few passages of introspection
where the past is referred to as if it were present. *Good
Morning Midnight*, on the other hand, bridges this
interval: it is a simultaneous narrative in the present
tense, where the moment of the story and the moment
of the narrating coincide. In Gérard Genette's terms,
'the rigorous simultaneousness of story and narrating
eliminates any sort of interference or temporal game'.[4]
Thus, narrating 'I' and narrated 'I' collide, establishing
Sasha – at least technically – as an integrated subject
producing an integrated text which she manages from
beginning to end, smoothly intermingling narrative and
interior monologue. We then expect to be dealing with a
highly homogeneous text with one single addresser in

command, and this in spite of the numerous time-shifts induced by Sasha's train of thought.

The feeling of immediacy and unity conveyed by the narrative strategy is checked, however, by quite a few jarring notes. Some of the past events Sasha remembers, for instance, expand into long sequences of retrospective narrating that seem to reintroduce the distance between narrating 'I' and narrated 'I', as in any other story told in retrospect and in the first person. One of these retrospective narratives is Sasha's disastrous interview with Mr Blank, the boss of the fashion shop where she used to work (*GMM*, 16–26). Apart from occasional use of the present tense, the whole sequence is told in the past. Similarly, most of Part Three, in which Sasha remembers her life with Enno, her former husband, is told in the past tense, and it is not until the last two pages of the unit (*GMM*, 120–1) that the text shifts back to Sasha's internalized conversation in the present. These long, embedded sequences of retrospective narrating come to disrupt the postulated unity of the narrative on the one hand and of the narrating instance on the other.

In addition to these long loops, dissonance may be observed at the level of the narrating time proper. More often than not, Sasha engages in a dialogue with herself, carefully planning out whatever she is about to say or undertake, arguing it out with herself, thus undermining the effect of spontaneity that one is entitled to expect from her narrative posture. One is struck by such lack of spontaneity when, at some point, two strangers come up to Sasha, abruptly asking her 'Pourquoi êtes-vous si triste?' (*GMM*, 39). Before she answers, she procrastinates, dithers, takes stock of her prospects, wondering which of the various possible answers would be the most adequate, regardless of the truth. Not only is the answer postponed at length, but the spoken

answer differs from the unuttered option she has finally
decided upon. The unending debate that never fails to
split the narrating self counteracts the effect of simultaneousness pertaining to the novel's narrative form.
Thus, every action Sasha takes is carefully pondered
over:

> Planning it all out. Eating. A movie. Eating again. One
> drink. A long walk back to the hotel. Bed. Luminal.
> Sleep. Just sleep – no dreams. (*GMM*, 15)

This fastidious programming is devised, on Sasha's part,
as a deliberate obliteration of anything that might betray
her singularity. Given the novel's narrative strategy
again, this is another paradox: autodiegetic narrative or
interior monologue are, by definition, egocentric forms,
grounded in the self, monitoring the subject's feelings,
impressions, memories, vision, and so on. *Good Morning
Midnight* subverts this conventional emphasis on the
private consciousness of individual selves. Sasha's self-
imposed routine, as it turns out, is entirely oriented
towards suppressing her idiosyncracies. The control she
exercises over her humdrum life is meant to channel, to
censor her inner self:

> But careful, careful! Don't get excited. You know
> what happens when you get excited and exalted,
> don't you? ... [...] So, no excitement. This is going to
> be a quiet, sane fortnight. (*GMM*, 14)

As is the case here, the supposedly integrated subject
that presides over simultaneous narrative and interior
monologue often forks into two voices, one censoring
the other, the extensive use of the second-person
pronoun signposting the split in Sasha's divided self.

Sasha may be determined to rub out the slight-
est incongruity in her appearance (*GMM*, 14) and to

circumvent any unruly manifestation of the self, but one of her dreams – for she does dream – reproduced at an early stage of the narrative (*GMM*, 12–13), reveals the fundamental tension that may account for this split. In her dream, she is walking in an overcrowded tube station where everybody seems to be going to the same place, following signs showing the way to some exhibition, while Sasha alone is looking for an exit. If this is a clear metaphor for her longing for difference, her wish remains unfulfilled. The dream culminates in the figure of her wounded father shouting 'Murder!', while Sasha, speechless at first, ends up repeating what her father says. Just as there is no escape route in the tube station, there is no deviating from what Mikhail Bakhtin calls 'ideologemes',[5] that is to say, words as reflections of a particular way of viewing the world, here embodied by the flow of pedestrians orchestrated by the signs printed in red letters and, of course, by the father-figure. Unless one kills the father, which Sasha does not, one cannot emancipate oneself from dialogue in the Bakhtinian sense of the word:

> On all its various routes toward the object, in all its directions, the word encounters an alien word and cannot help encountering it in a living, tension-filled interaction.[6]

Sasha's is, in Mikhail Bakhtin's words, an 'Adamic dream', for '[o]nly the mythical Adam, who approached a virginal and as yet verbally unqualified world with the first word, could really have escaped from start to finish this dialogic inter-orientation with the alien word that occurs in the object'.[7] Sasha is not Adam, nor is she Eve; she can only follow the path along which the word is continually encountering someone else's word. The text itself follows the same path for, Sasha's dream echoing

Hamlet, the passage may also be seen as a self-reflexive representation of intertextuality: not unlike Sasha, it is entangled in someone else's text.

Enmeshed in second-hand words, the true self is nowhere to be found in the monologue. Sasha eloquently spells out this ostensible disappearance in a flashback recounting her remembered suicide attempt:

> I have no pride – no pride, no name, no face, no country. I don't belong anywhere. Too sad, too sad.... It doesn't matter, there I am, like one of those straws which floats round the edge of a whirlpool and is gradually sucked into the centre, the dead centre, where everything is stagnant, everything is calm. (*GMM*, 38)

What seems to be speaking in Sasha's text is a set of discursive matrixes that absorb the subject, as this whirlpool sucks up the straw-like self towards a point where it is left with no identity or substance. Thus Sasha's utterances seem to be produced by a depersonalized 'I', an anonymous self in which other voices ceaselessly reverberate. The autodiegetic narrator is far removed from any notion of a psychological self whose singularity the narrative sets out to explore; it is rather a crossroads where heterogeneous utterances intersect, an anonymous space where different discursive practices interact: '[e]very word I say has chains round its ankles; every thought I think is weighted with heavy weights' (*GMM*, 88).

Parodic Expertise

Although this obsessional intertextuality acts as a check upon self-expression, Sasha tends to exploit it rather than resist it. Her relationship to language is organized mainly around two conscious operations, observation and quotation. It is through these operations, controlled by Sasha, that heterogeneous utterances are incorporated into her discourse, where, however, they remain heterogeneous in the sense that they are not entirely assimilated by the text. Sasha consistently distances herself from language or from certain discursive practices, and even if she somehow absorbs and transforms the borrowed utterances, giving them, as we shall see, a new semantic orientation, the distance always remains. Were it not for the various sequences in which Sasha, contrary to the earlier heroines, proves to be an expert speaker, this distancing might have posited Sasha as a defective one. Instead, it converts language into an object of inquiry ironically scrutinized by a knowledgeable heroine.

One of Sasha's distinctive features is indeed her command of social and linguistic codes. Some of the flashbacks bear witness to her past difficulty in coming to terms with the prescribed codes – see, for instance, her making no sense of the absurdly obscure cipher of the cash-register in the shop called Young Britain (*GMM*, 26) – but, even at the time, she has no trouble identifying them. Despite her younger years and lack of experience, then, Sasha recognizes social types and shows remarkable competence in portraying them. Mr Blank, to name but one, is 'the real English type, le businessman' (*GMM*, 17). The French definite article humorously underlines the taxonomic process which, as it should, follows from rigorous observation of phenomena: '[b]owler-hat, majestic trousers, oh-my-God expression, ha-ha eyes – I know him at once' (*GMM*, 17). With the same remarkable insight, she can tell in the twinkle of an eye that one of the young Russians who is striking up conversation with her is an optimist (*GMM*, 47).

If Sasha is very good at identifying social or
psychological types, her linguistic expertise is equally,
if not more, manifest. For instance, she detects a stylistic
error in a conversation she overhears in Theodore's
restaurant where she is having lunch: ' "Et qu'est-ce
qu'elle fout ici, maintenant?" ' (*GMM*, 43). Sasha
expertly comments upon the mistake, corrects it and
kindly provides an annotated translation, paying attention to register of language and connotation:

> But what language! Considering the general get-up
> what you should have said was: 'Qu'est-ce qu'elle
> fiche ici?' (*GMM*, 44)

> Qu'est-ce qu'elle fout ici, la vieille? What the devil
> (translating it politely) is she doing here, that old
> woman? What is she doing here, the stranger, the
> alien, the old one? (*GMM*, 46)

If Sasha shies away from language as a means of self-
expression, she is found willing to make extensive use of
metalanguage, that is to say, technical language dealing
with the properties of language. There is an early
suggestion of this leaning of hers, albeit to a lesser
degree, in the opening lines of the novel, where Sasha
describes the hotel room she is moving into and the
adjoining street:

> There are two beds, a big one for madame and a
> smaller one on the opposite side for monsieur. [...]
> It is a large room, the smell of cheap hotels faint,
> almost imperceptible. The street outside is [...] what
> they call an impasse. (*GMM*, 9)

By nature, as Philippe Hamon demonstrates in his study
of description in narrative prose, description partakes of

metalanguage. It can be defined as a '*texte de savoir*' in which the implied author or addresser of the description exhibits his knowledge of the text (the description is where 'clues' to what is coming next are dropped) as well as his knowledge of the world and of its codes.[8] Thus the act of describing effects a temporary withdrawal from self-expressive speech and a foregrounding of the describer's metalinguistic ability to classify, organize and control textual material.[9] In the initial description of her hotel room, Sasha's private voice withdraws, giving way to a more impersonal mode in order to make show of an encyclopedic knowledge of the world and of its uses. She relates her room to the paradigmatic hotel room, exhibits her knowledge of the codes of matrimony and, in so doing, appeals to the reader's own competence, referring him to the common text of culture. While this exhibition of knowledge may invest Sasha with discursive authority, it also brings to light the essentially intertextual dimension of description which, Philippe Hamon argues, must be considered as the site of a rewriting. This is corroborated by the etymological root of the word: *de-scribere* means 'to write from a model'.[10] When Sasha mentions the two beds, she is in fact designating herself in the process of quoting from some prior textualization, the set of conventions in use at the time. Intertextuality is brought into relief by the import of French words, the interference of two languages spotlighting the correlation of texts that informs any description. With the last words, 'what they call an impasse', Sasha conspicuously gives up speech, relocating the origin of discourse in the anonymous, collective addresser of another text.

As early as the incipit then, Sasha's relation to language seems to be on the side of metalanguage, language being looked at from a critical distance. That Sasha's detached gaze should be prominent in a descriptive passage is, after all, only natural, for the act of describing is necessarily performed by a beholding 'I'/eye. Less predictably, however, this critical detachment can also be traced in a dialogue involving Sasha and the two young Russians she has just met (*GMM*, 40–1). Instead of recording what is being said in direct speech, Sasha processes the whole scene in a kind of paraphrase ranging from summary to indirect speech. The utterance 'I say that I'm not sad' (*GMM*, 40), for instance, where 'I'm not sad' might have been expected, comes as a surprise within the framework of a dialogue. It is as if Sasha were an eye-witness to the conversation rather than a participant in it. Not only does she disengage herself from the dialogue but, more surprisingly, from her own words too. The paradoxical addition of the reporting clause ('I say that'), which is at odds with both the use of the present tense and Sasha's actual participation in the conversation, is suggestive of a split in the speaking subject and undermines the feeling of (relative) immediacy usually associated with quoted, straightforward dialogue.

For all this distancing and disengagement from the dialogue, Sasha as enunciating subject does not altogether disappear from the discursive stage. The various marks of her distancing read as symptoms of a parodic reworking of a highly conventional scene, a kind of conversation piece aptly entitled 'the usual conversation' (*GMM*, 40), a parodic reworking through which the subject, despite its self-effacing strategies, returns with a vengeance. The object of the sequence is not so much the rendering of a meeting between Sasha and two strangers as the self-referential representation of discursive practices which Sasha parodies with much self-irony. When, for instance, she boasts about her 'many friends' (*GMM*, 40), or poses as the deep person possessed of some essential truth about mankind – 'I look into the distance with a blank expression and say: "Human beings are cruel – horribly cruel" ' (*GMM*, 41) – she is not referring to any personal, traumatic experience; the pomposity of the utterance and of the stage business is out of character where Sasha is concerned. More to the point, she is self-consciously dramatizing the fact that she is performing conversational rituals. This parodic mimicry deflects the focus away from content to lay the emphasis on form. Characteristically, the substance of the conversation is reduced to a series of mere headlines: they discuss 'love', 'cruelty' and, Sasha ironically notes, 'sheer off politics' (*GMM*, 41). If the gist of the conversation is dismissively skimmed over, Sasha dwells upon the even more trivial things the three characters say when about to part. Her lingering over such insignificant content directs the reader's attention to form and may be seen as an index of Sasha's parodic intent. Again, the dialogue is entirely revisited by her, as the closing paragraph shows:

> Well, we'll meet again, shan't we?...Of course we shall. It would be a pity not to meet again, wouldn't it? Will I meet them at the Pékin tomorrow for lunch? I have an idea that I shan't be feeling much like Chinese food at half-past twelve tomorrow. We arrange to meet at the Dôme at four o'clock. (*GMM*, 41)

These lines highlight the increasingly revisionary hand Sasha has in the transcription of the dialogue. In the first three sentences, she uses a mode akin to free direct speech as speech tags like 'he says' or 'I say' are deleted. Although this could be indicative of an unintrusive narrator who reports things in a straightforward manner, the omission of the quotation marks displaces the origin of discourse: it is hard to decide whether this is actual dialogue or Sasha's stream of consciousness. In the fourth sentence, she adopts free indirect speech. In any other context, one could say that free indirect speech gives the illusion of intimate access to a character's mind, narratorial participation being kept to a minimum. Yet, because it comes after direct speech, however altered, free indirect speech denotes stronger narratorial involvement in the transcription. Finally, in the last two sentences, Sasha returns to the narrative mode, thus taking full 'authorial' responsibility for the utterances. In the course of the paragraph, Sasha's enunciation creeps more and more into the revised dialogue.

The passage falls in with the structure of parody as Linda Hutcheon defines it:

> parody is a sophisticated genre in the demands it makes on its practitioners and its interpreters. The encoder, then the decoder, must effect a structural superimposition of texts that incorporates the old into the new. Parody is a bitextual synthesis.[11]

The sequence is indeed a 'bitextual synthesis', super-imposing two texts: the three characters' small talk and Sasha's revision of it. In her parodic text, Sasha mimics the ritual formulae people resort to on taking their leave, while critically reworking this preformed material. Her systematic rephrasing of the dialogue makes for the synthetic coexistence of discursive practices and of a metalanguage. She applies and simultaneously distances herself from set formulae, thus illustrating the fundamental ambivalence of parody: '[w]hile the act and form of parody are those of incorporation, its function is one of separation and contrast'.[12] Parody is 'repetition, but repetition that includes difference'.[13] Sasha's 'transcontextualiz-ing' gaze engineers a dethroning of discursive models through ambivalent mimicry. This critical aping may also be observed in her use of quotation.

Quotation

Autodiegetic narrating tends to establish Sasha's text as production, and yet her constant borrowing from previous texts tends to identify it as reproduction. She ceaselessly delegates speech to other 'authors' and, significantly, it is with one of those delegations that the novel starts. The heroine entrusts her hotel room with the task of providing the first sentence of her narrative: '"Quite like old times", the room says. "Yes? No?"' (*GMM*, 9). Because of this tendency to quote all the time, one is tempted to see her text as sheer repetition of other texts, this mimicry reflecting her inability to coin her own words within masculine discourse. In the act of quoting, however, the delegation of speech is not complete; the subject who quotes from other people's discourse is not altogether unobtrusive. As is the case with parody, quotation is 'trans-contextualized repeti-tion',[14] in other words, repetition with difference, although the critical distancing that defines parody is not necessarily implicit in the idea of quotation in general or Sasha's practice of it in particular. Sometimes, the borrowed fragment is a vicarious means for her to express her own feelings about something. She might leave it to somebody else to say it but one feels that Sasha is indeed speaking through the other's voice, as when she quotes from *Lady Windermere's Fan*, for example: '"The laughter, the horrible laughter of the world – a thing more tragic than all the tears the world has ever shed...."' (*GMM*, 115). Were it not for her general avoidance of self-exposure, Sasha could have said this in her own words. In this particular instance, quotation partakes of her dissembling and the quotation marks are mere screens affording false distance. Sometimes, however, they are indicative of critical detachment, a detachment which should not be mistaken for an eclipse of the speaking subject. Through 'trans-contextualization' and critical distancing, Sasha steps in to provide implicit evaluation of the borrowed piece. The following passage illustrates the tension between assimilation and dissimulation common to parody and quotation:

> 'At first I was afraid they would let gates bang on my hindquarters, and I used to be nervous of unknown people and places'. Quotation from *The Autobiography of a Mare* – one of my favourite books. . . . We English are so animal-conscious. We know so instinctively what the creatures feel and why they feel it. . . . (*GMM*, 37)

The sequence is made up of two quotations: the first one is an acknowledged borrowing complete with indication of source and quotation marks. Although this inscribed indebtedness acts as a distancing device, the semantic content effects a lessening of the distance between Sasha and the borrowed utterance: the mare ostensibly voices feelings that she shares. In the second quotation, taken from collective discourse this time, conventional demarcation has vanished. This may suggest that Sasha plainly appropriates the heterogeneous utterance, but this is in fact where repetition with difference comes in. Her parodic mimicry of collective discourse is signalled by the suspension points that frame the quote and read as markers of irony. Thus the act of quoting by which the speaker seems to be relinquishing speech paradoxically is an active recycling, that bestows an added sense of importance upon the borrower's *énonciation*. Like parody, quoting consists of the simultaneous activation of two texts and is poised on an unstable borderline between plain assimilation of the borrowed text and plain relinquishment of speech.

As a rule, quoting contributes much to the ironic dimension of the novel. Sasha's discreet editing of the borrowed text results in an exhibition of discourse which, under Sasha's ironic scrutiny, becomes less referential than self-referential. By nature, quoting tends to exhibit language as object. As Antoine Compagnon explains,[15] there are two stages in the act of quoting, each positing language as object: the first one is an underlining of the unit to be borrowed; one borrows a given discursive unit because its form has drawn one's attention. After the reader's response to enticing form comes the grafting process: the quoted fragment is a foreign body, a linguistic object one appropriates. In addition to the 'natural' self-reflexive dimension of quotation, the graft does not take in *Good Morning Midnight* – it is as if one could see the scars – and faulty incorporation tends to make this exhibition of language even more conspicuous. In any case, quoting is a component part of Sasha's metalanguage. A good example of this self-referential aspect is a sentence borrowed from Sidonie, a subsidiary character who, we gather, has lent Sasha the money to spend a fortnight in Paris: '[b]ut one mustn't put everything on the same plane. That's her great phrase' (*GMM*, 12). Sidonie's phrase is grafted on to Sasha's text, not woven into it. Coming without contextual detail, the quoted unit remains other and its heterogeneity is reinforced by Sasha's critical reading, for she moves on to a sort of textual analysis of Sidonie's utterance, translating it, assessing its semantic implications, and so on. Again, Sasha emerges as an expert reader and as her

metalinguistic competence is once more brought to the
fore, our attention is directed to a discursive mode. In
the same way as Sidonie's discourse creates determinations within which Sasha feels she is caught (Sidonie's
idea of what Sasha's 'plane' is), Sasha's use of quotation
creates a prejudicial mirroring process in which language is caught.

The heterogeneity of the borrowings is sustained by
their position in the narrative. Being mostly found in
embedded flashbacks, the borrowed fragments are
doubly distanced, through Sasha's critical stance and
through time. If this almost systematic embedding
confirms the narrator's adverse detachment, it also
bears witness to the narrative's obsession with repetition,
which is the organizing principle of the plot of *Good
Morning Midnight*. Returning to Paris, Sasha moves into
charted territory where known places and people keep
reminding her of a haunting past. Quotation as
repetition of previous texts chimes with the novel's
preoccupation with repeat performances, a good illustration of which is provided by the following sequence,
where Sasha recollects and quotes an old friend of hers
who tried to pass himself off as a music lover:

> Bach, of course, was his favourite composer. The
> others, he said, he preferred to read, not to listen to.
> 'Heard melodies are sweet, but those unheard are
> sweeter' – that sort of thing. (*GMM*, 34–5)

This passage exemplifies the way in which the text
moves from repetition to repetition: Sasha's text
reproduces another text which, in turn, borrows from
Keats's *Ode on a Grecian Urn*. Keats's line is reified in the
process, all the more so as it is emptied of meaning by
the young man's posturing. The latter is not mobilizing
the intrinsic significance of the line so much as the

authority of the cultural reference in an attempt to impress people. One would therefore be tempted to say that the sequences of retrospective narrating are primarily meant to dramatize discursive modes. Instead of using language to represent past events, Sasha tends to use past events in order to represent language. The role of such subsidiary characters as Sidonie or this nameless young man is to provide discursive material for Sasha to study. Repeating what others say or have said, she engages in a laying-bare of speech or writing as repetition.

Clichés and Commonplaces

For Antoine Compagnon quotation is the model for all writing: writing is always rewriting and, as such, approximates to quotation.[16] Through her extensive use of quotation, Sasha tends to equate speaking with quoting, suggesting that any speaker, especially a woman who cannot but borrow from masculine discourse, is necessarily entangled in interdiscursive relationships that turn discourse into mimicry and repetition. As well as uncovering this essential intertextuality, Sasha's exploration of discursive practices tends to expose language itself as an exhausted form. This exposure is carried out through her constant borrowing from a wide range of hackneyed expressions, clichés and stereotypes. Her reworking of a well-known line from Racine's *Phèdre*, 'Vénus toute entière à sa proie attachée' (*GMM*, 68), is emblematic of the undermining at work in Sasha's use of quotation. 'Trans-contextualizing' the line, she divests it of its distinguished attire to have it take on a cruder meaning: in the present circumstances, the line serves to describe a gigolo's assiduous attentions. In the context of

Racine's tragedy, the metaphor, if not very original, is not quite a cliché. Its lack of originality has its source in the classical belief in the value of imitation and Racine's use of this essentially decorative, unoriginal trope mainly testifies to his complying with the recommended imitation of the normative forms and elevated style of noble literature. Misquoted in a less dignified context, applied to René who, Sasha suspects, is out to squeeze some money out of her, Racine's metaphor is ironically downgraded into a clichéd literary phrase, both hackneyed and vulgar, for, having lost its original polish, it leaves the field of classical tragedy to enter that of low comedy.

The 'trans-contextualization' of Racine's line partakes of Sasha's critical stance *vis-à-vis* discursive models which are made to appear as the breeding ground of ossified forms, be it clichés or stereotyped modes of thinking. Thus Sasha seems to take great pleasure in jotting down the commonplaces that pepper ordinary conversations overheard here and there:

> 'Life is difficult', the Arab says.
> 'Yes, life isn't easy', the girl says.
> Long pause.
> 'One needs a lot of courage, to live', the Arab says.
> 'Ah, I believe you', the girl says, shaking her head and clicking her tongue. (*GMM*, 14)

This time, and contrary to her conversation with the two Russians, the dialogue is not at all revisited by Sasha. Only the tags and the lean descriptive elements reminiscent of stage directions betray the narrator's presence. But the ironic effect is derived precisely from this plain monitoring. As Sasha bluntly shows in this ostensibly non-committal recording, no major breakthrough is achieved in this flagging conversation which

seems to mobilize only the phatic function of language – if even that, for Sasha is careful to monitor
the long pauses between the trite remarks. Elsewhere,
remembering the time when she attended the funeral of
Anatole France, she dramatizes herself in the process of
'paying him the tribute of a last salute' with her husband
(*GMM*, 15). In the context, through the discrepancy
between the very formal style of the utterance and the
attendants' behaviour, the idiomatic phrase is made to
appear as a cliché. Its relative pomposity is ironically
pitted against the all but meditative attitude of the
people in the funeral procession, who are all paying
Anatole France the tribute of a last salute while
frivolously chatting away and making dates for various
social events. The discrepancy lends an insight into the
nature of cliché. Through excessive use – and the
phrase is indeed repeated three times in the space of a
few lines – the original significance of the idiom has
weakened and it is now being circulated as a meaningless set expression, as lifeless as Anatole France. The
passage reads as an archaeology of cliché, a replica of the
ossifying repetition from which cliché proceeds.

This episode throws light on to one of the main
features of cliché, its 'sociality'. If quotation and cliché
both are borrowings from previous texts, quotation
interrelates two individual discursive units while cliché,
collectively authored, tends to connect the borrowed
unit with collective discourse and its social backdrop,
highlighting the fact that there is no such thing as
private property in the field of language, that everything
is socialized. As a conservative linguistic manifestation of
communal consensus, cliché falls prey to the negative
evaluation which generally affects the representatives of
the law and of the dominant idiom in Jean Rhys's texts.
As Helen Carr puts it, 'Rhys's protagonists are acutely
aware that the social machine is kept in place by a use of

language which ignores nuance, complexity, deviation, ambivalence, a language which reiterates the fetishistic phrases which preserve the status quo.'[17] In the world of those Sasha calls 'the extremely respectable', everything, she complains, 'is born out of a cliché, rests on a cliché, survives by a cliché. And they believe in the clichés – there's no hope' (*GMM*, 36). Rescued from emotional drowning by her respectable family five years before, Sasha, who came to depend on their clichés, felt as if she was being buried alive: '[t]he lid of the coffin shut down with a bang' (*GMM*, 37). Thus, the condition for becoming integrated seems to be this mimicry of pre-existing formulae which, it turns out, is a form of death, with cliché – often a *dead* metaphor – as an index of lethal conservatism. Moving along the beaten tracks of experience and discourse, one can only reach lifeless exhaustion, and moving along beaten tracks is just what Sasha does, however reluctantly, in Paris. Returning to the site of her earlier drowning, she is haunted by repetition, metaphorically walking to the singsong rhythm of some old song: '[t]he gramophone record is going strong in my head: "Here this happened, here that happened..."' (*GMM*, 15). Only once and only for a time did Sasha escape the obsessive replay of the same old song when she gave birth to a baby who unfortunately would not live for more than a few days. Then, Sasha and the midwife who attends to her speak 'a language that is no language' (*GMM*, 50). This escape is a short-lived one for, after the baby's death and thanks to the bandages in which the nurse swathes her, Sasha is just as she were before, 'without one line, without one wrinkle, without one crease' (*GMM*, 52).

One may wonder whether this borrowing from the common stock of clichés signifies the death of the individual speaking subject. It does not, as long as there is evidence of a critical distancing on Sasha's part.

Exhibiting the lifeless forms between quotation marks or through any other distancing device, designating them as foreign bodies, she simultaneously delineates her own territory and asserts her singularity, for the speaking subject is always present in the ironic code, although there may be no or few tangible signs of his/her presence. However, the ironic code is not the only way in which Sasha relates to clichés. In accordance with her determination to conform, to have 'a quiet, sane fortnight' (*GMM*, 14), she seems to be willing to surrender to pre-existing discourse and to comply univocally with the law of cliché. This non-critical appropriation of previous texts comes to light in a sequence where Sasha borrows from but uncritically incorporates the jargon of hoteliers:

> A room. A nice room. A beautiful room. A beautiful room with bath. A very beautiful room with bath. A bedroom and sitting-room with bath. Up to the dizzy heights of the suite. Two bedrooms, sitting-room, bath and vestibule. (The small bedroom is in case you don't feel like me, or in case you meet somebody you like better and come in late.) Anything you want brought up on the dinner-wagon. (But, alas! the waiter has a louse on his collar. What is that on his collar?... Bitte schön, mein Herr, bitte schön....) Swing high.... Now, slowly, down. A beautiful room with bath. A room with bath. A nice room. A room.... (*GMM*, 29)

It could be argued that this passage is yet another testimony of Sasha's ironic detachment. Indeed, excessive repetition results in a kind of overstatement which could be suggestive of the subject's ironic recycling. More to the point, and in spite of the potentially ironic utterances in brackets, the passage encapsulates Sasha's compliance with compulsory mimicry. Here, she is no longer observing linguistic phenomena in a dismissive manner; she exploits the expressive value of these phrases to sum up her life and its ups and downs, also reflected in the almost visual, up-and-down structure of the paragraph. There is a kind of morbid jubilation in these variations on the hotel room, all the more so as the systematic listing of the variants suggests that difference is an illusion: the paragraph retraces its footsteps, so to speak, starting and ending with 'a room'; the variant is cancelled out in sameness. If irony is still active here, its task is no longer to assert the subject's difference but to expose sameness masquerading as difference. The same misery can be detected whatever the circumstances: although the luxury suite evinces material ease, it also reveals the married woman's condition of beggary and her subservience to her husband's good will. Moreover, the prestige of the suite is somewhat tainted by the louse on the waiter's collar and, as Sasha will finally conclude, '[a]ll rooms are the same' (*GMM*, 33). What she exposes through her mimicry is the levelling power of the patriarchal order which forces one into repetition. The hotel room, a metonymy for its preordained hierarchy, functions as an emblem and a reminder of repetition since, in the question it puts to Sasha in the novel's incipit, it establishes the present as repetition of the past. As a symbol of anonymity, it may also be held to signify the disappearance of the individual speaking subject, eclipsed by an atopic, collective addresser.

If, from a very early stage, repetition proves to be the organizing principle of Sasha's life as well as of this text 'saturated with the past' (*GMM*, 91), a few pages before the novel's conclusion, it sounds as if Sasha could still find a way out of it and make her destiny branch off. Being faced with a choice between returning to life, however painfully, or staying within the reassuring routine of mortiferous repetition, Sasha seems to go deliberately for the second option. As she is about to go to bed with René, experiencing the painful awakening of desire and hope, she seals the doom of their relationship, hurting his feelings in a self-defensive attempt to make him leave before she comes to life. As René finally walks out on her, she ends up having sex with a man she loathes, her abject next-door neighbour whom she calls the 'ghost of the landing' (*GMM*, 13). It is not clear whether Sasha *deliberately* surrenders to this spectre of repetition who reappears no less than six times in the course of the narrative,[18] for the passage harbours one of the most excruciating instances of self-division. While, out loud, Sasha spares no pains to humiliate René, casting him into the role of a begging gigolo who lives off mercenary sex, Sasha silently implores him to stay. It is as if she were being forced to articulate words from which she is alienated, forced, that is, into self-abasing repetition, symbolized by the neighbour she keeps running into who, described as 'a paper man' (*GMM*, 31), may be seen as one of those pre-existing texts which compel the subject's utterances. The final 'yes' that marks Sasha's surrender has often been likened to Molly Bloom's 'yes' in the monologue which closes *Ulysses*, and it is hardly surprising that Jean Rhys's ultimate acknowledgement of the tyranny of repetition should be carried out through intertextual reference. It must be added that while Joyce's reworking of Homer's Penelope is repetition with difference – Molly is not nearly as faithful as Penelope – Jean Rhys seems to rule out any deviation from repetitive patterns by having René leave and throwing Sasha into the arms of a recurring ghost.

Through the tension between individual expression, postulated by *Good Morning Midnight's* affinity with interior monologue, and unavoidable parrotry, materialized in the constant borrowings from all kinds of pre-existing texts, Jean Rhys represents a crisis within the speaking subject, especially the female one upon whom mimicry is imposed. As well as delineating the condition of women as speakers, *Good Morning Midnight* may also be defining literary discourse as repetition of other texts. The most telling representation of this dialogical condition is the remembered episode in which Sasha is commissioned by a rich lady in Antibes to write fairy-tales. Thus, Sasha becomes a ghost writer who, as such, must obey strict rules drastically curbing her own creative contribution. Having to deal with one of the most highly coded genres, Sasha is moreover given strict directions as to thematic content, when she is not provided with the opening sentence of the tale she is to write (*GMM*, 139). After a few tries, she is kindly requested to alter her style, the ultimate stronghold of the subject, as her employer, who disapproves of her taste for monosyllabics and wants to get her money's worth, demands that she use longer words in future:

> Long words. Chiaroscuro? Translucent? . . . I bet he'd like cataclysmal action and centrifugal flux, but the point is how can I get them into a Persian garden? . . . Well, I might. Stranger things have happened. (*GMM*, 140)

It took Jean Rhys over twenty-five years to solve the problem Sasha is faced with here, namely to produce a text that she somehow can call hers despite the various constraints that pre-shape it. It took Jean Rhys over twenty-five years before she could rearrange preordained material into a text over which she could claim copyright. Meanwhile, *Good Morning Midnight* stands out as a 'mosaic of quotations' and dramatizes the fact that, in J. Hillis Miller's words, a literary text 'is inhabited [...] by a long chain of parasitical presences, echoes, allusions, guests, ghosts of previous texts'.[19]

7 *Wide Sargasso Sea*: The Woman's Text

In *Good Morning Midnight*, Jean Rhys suggests that the feminine steers a precarious course between repetition, at best parodic, and silence. At first sight, *Wide Sargasso Sea* is still caught in the mesh of repetitive patterns, if only because it is a rewriting of *Jane Eyre*. Jean Rhys's last novel, published in 1966, is an extended version of the story of the first Mrs Rochester, the mad Creole locked up in the attic of Thornfield Hall. It seems, however, that some twenty-seven years after the publication of *Good Morning Midnight*, repetition is no longer the curse it used to be, and one has the feeling that it is within the intertextual game that Jean Rhys finds a voice for the feminine to speak out loud, that it is within repetition that emancipation is achieved. The title of the novel[1] encapsulates this creative use of repetition. As well as roughly indicating where the story is set (the Sargasso Sea lies north-east of the Lesser West Indies), 'Wide Sargasso Sea' also points to the problematic of the novel. The Sargasso Sea is named after the seaweed that accumulates in that becalmed area because of eddying currents. Forming a large, intricate mesh on the surface which makes sailing perilous and causes many shipwrecks, the sargassos may be seen as an apt figure for stagnation and deadly repetitive patterns. The Sargasso Sea may then be regarded as a magnified version of the 'dead centre' of the vortex of *Good Morning Midnight* which leaves the subject with 'no pride, no name, no face, no country' (*GMM*, 38). On the other hand, being one of the places where eels return each year to lay their eggs, the Sargasso Sea is also a strategic site as far as the natural rhythms of regeneration are concerned. In its dormant waters, repetition has a creative function; both lethal and fecund, the Sargasso Sea is the seat of cyclical renewal, of creation within repetition.

Trapped in the Meshes of the Sargassos

At the end of *Good Morning Midnight*, Sasha surrenders to repetition, embodied in 'the ghost of the landing'. There is a strong suggestion that the spectre of repetition returns to haunt Jean Rhys's last novel, an earlier version of which she had planned to entitle 'Le revenant', as she says in one of her letters.[2] 'Le revenant' is Jean Rhys's metaphorical inscription of a pre-existing discourse which compels a woman's text, turning it into an echo-chamber.

The text is first of all subject to internal repetition. *Wide Sargasso Sea* is a multi-voiced narrative with several narrators: the first part is told by Antoinette, who recounts her childhood and adolescence in Jamaica; in Part Two, her unnamed husband takes over, describing his arrival in the West Indies and the honeymoon at Granbois, with a nine-page section again narrated by Antoinette (*WSS*, 89–98); at the beginning of Part Three, a heterodiegetic narrator reports a conversation between Grace Poole and Leah, characters borrowed from *Jane Eyre*, followed by Grace Poole's monologue, until Antoinette again speaks in the first person. From the point of view of structure, *Wide Sargasso Sea* is a mosaic of narratives which, at times, complement each other and, at others, repeat each other. Daniel Cosway's letter to Antoinette's husband (*WSS*, 79–82), which plays a decisive role in the drama, is partly a doubling of Antoinette's account of her childhood with her mother.

When, moreover, she undertakes to demonstrate that Cosway's letter is sheer slander, what she says in order to prove her case is yet another echo of Part One. These repetitions with variations which present different versions of the same events foster the relativity pertaining to multi-voiced narratives, but internal repetition can also be seen as a reflection of 'external' repetition, namely the intertextual relationship between *Wide Sargasso Sea* and *Jane Eyre*, which tends to establish Jean Rhys's protagonists as carbon copies of an earlier cast.

The preordained quality of their destiny is duplicated in the novel's extensive use of anticipation. As Gérard Genette explains, anticipation is common practice in autodiegetic narratives:

> The 'first-person' narrative lends itself better than any other to anticipation, by the very fact of its avowedly retrospective character, which authorizes the narrator to allude to the future and in particular to his present situation, for these form part of his role.[3]

If anticipation is in line with *Wide Sargasso Sea*'s narrative strategy, it seems to me that it makes for the inscription of fate in the narrative, locking the characters within a 'plot of predestination', to use the formula Tzvetan Todorov applies to Homeric narrative.[4] The text is shot through with premonitions or forebodings and the characters are invested with a vague knowledge of what is awaiting them. The male narrator, for instance, puzzles over his 'confused impressions' (*WSS*, 64), is on several occasions plagued with misgivings or feels he is being warned of something (*WSS*, 60), in what seems to be an adaptation of tragic foreboding. When fate strikes through the agency of Daniel Cosway, whose letter will poison the honeymoon, 'Rochester'[5] admits: 'I felt no surprise. It was as if I'd expected it, been waiting for it' (*WSS*, 82).

The various premonitions are supplemented by what Gérard Genette calls 'repeating prolepses', anticipations referring 'in advance to an event that will be told in full in its place'.[6] These prolepses should not be confused with 'mere *advance mentions*, simple markers without anticipation, even an allusive anticipation, which will acquire their significance only later on and which belong to the completely classic art of "preparation" '.[7] The text is full of 'advance notices', Genette's alternative formula for prolepsis, creating expectations in the reader's mind which in all cases will be fulfilled either immediately or in the long run. That the anticipatory hints should invariably be followed by resolution establishes the narrative as a prophetic one, in much the same way as any tragedy. The passage preceding the adulterous scene with Amélie in Part Two illustrates this prophetic dimension:

> I sat on the bed waiting, for I knew that Amélie would come and I knew what she would say: 'I am sorry for you'.
> She came soundlessly on bare feet. 'I get you something to eat', she said. [...] Then she said, 'I am sorry for you'. (*WSS*, 115)

Amélie says the expected words and, just as predictably, 'Rochester' will have sex with her. Then all he has to do is to wait and listen for Antoinette's predictable departure, which does not fail to occur (*WSS*, 116). All of his predictions, or prophecies should one say, come true, so much so that the whole of the plot seems to be proceeding from pre-existing discourse (the various prophecies). Within a 'plot of predestination', the staged event always follows in the wake of previous discourse, thus being made to appear as the repeating actualization of discourse. Prophecy inevitably generates repetition.

Caught in this 'plot of predestination', Antoinette and 'Rochester' have no creative power over their lives.

'Star-crossed lovers', they are puppets in the clutches of a tragic *fatum*, trapped in multifarious determinisms. Marrying Antoinette, 'Rochester' is by no means creating his own story. As a penniless younger son, he is pressurized by his family into an arranged marriage with a presumably wealthy Creole. After the wedding, in acknowledgement of his subjection, he reluctantly writes to his father: '[a]ll is well and has gone according to your plans and wishes' (*WSS*, 63). Remembering the day when he was first introduced to his wife-to-be, he lucidly remarks: 'I played the part I was expected to play' (*WSS*, 64). Generally speaking, and as a testimony of the fated quality of his tragic life, 'Rochester' proves extremely susceptible to the influence of others, especially of Daniel Cosway, whose function is to initiate the tragic process by transforming 'Rochester's' feeling of estrangement into hatred. After receiving his letter filled with scandalous revelations about Antoinette's family, 'Rochester' decides to pay a visit to him and is strangely mesmerized by the man, unable to move or to undo the tragic spell (*WSS*, 103). Listening to Cosway's slanderous spate of words, he opens out to hatred and tragic repetition, for it is under Cosway's embittered aegis that he becomes the double of *Jane Eyre*'s Rochester. From then on, he can only watch Antoinette sink into madness, and prepare for the passage back to Thornfield Hall where he will shut her up. Hearsay, itself a form of repetition, begets a hateful creature and a *doppelgänger*. Now a 'revenant', a reincarnation of Edward Fairfax Rochester, Jean Rhys's male character prophetically sketches a blueprint for Bertha's cell:

> I drew a house surrounded by trees. A large house. I divided the third floor into rooms and in one room I drew a standing woman. (*WSS*, 134)

Although 'Rochester' is the architect of the house and seems to originate it, his sketch foreshadows nothing but a repetition: it is the echo of another text, of an already inhabited house (of fiction).

Antoinette is likewise locked in an eddy of compelling determinations. One of them is Caribbean social history, as Coral Ann Howells points out:

> Hated by the blacks and despised for their poverty by both blacks and other whites, Antoinette and her mother are the victims of a system [the plantation system] the collapse of which has not only dispossessed them as a class but also deprived them as individuals of any means of independent survival.[8]

Blood forms another pattern of determinism. Antoinette cannot unknot family ties and, as the story unfolds, she looks more and more like her mother. Their physical likeness is underlined on many occasions: Antoinette comes to have the same frown as her mother, which, in both cases, looks as if it had 'been cut with a knife' (*WSS*, 17, 114). The destiny of the daughter repeats that of the mother: both marry an Englishman and both end up sinking into alcoholism and madness. Daniel Cosway brings out the similarities in his letter and calls 'Rochester's' attention to the fact that Antoinette is 'going the same way as her mother' (*WSS*, 83). At the end of Part Two, 'Rochester' spells out the identification of the two women, echoing Cosway's words: '[t]ied to a lunatic for life – a drunken lying lunatic – gone her mother's way' (*WSS*, 135).

In an attempt perhaps to bring the curse of genealogy to an end, 'Rochester', having found out that Antoinette was named after her mother (*WSS*, 94), decides to call her Bertha. Ironically, as he is trying to undo one filiation, he creates another, this time between *Wide*

Sargasso Sea and Charlotte Brontë's novel. Either way, Antoinette is part of a lineage of madwomen. Calling his wife Bertha, symbolically breaking the ties of blood, 'Rochester' engenders the double of *Jane Eyre*'s mad wife, creating repetition just when he thought he could avert it. Antoinette is thus thrown into a new set of equally coercive determinations, those pertaining to intertextual links. Although Jean Rhys makes significant alterations to Charlotte Brontë's account of Edward Rochester's first marriage, especially by shifting the perspective, she cannot entirely emancipate herself from the plot of *Jane Eyre*. Her letters provide evidence that she never really sought to in the first place:

> It might be possible to unhitch the whole thing from Charlotte Brontë's novel, but I don't want to do that. It is that particular Creole I want to write about, not any of the other mad Creoles.[9]

Wide Sargasso Sea borrows a lot of narrative material from the matrix novel. The motives for the arranged marriage are similar: 'Rochester' finds himself thrust into an alien culture for financial reasons, while Antoinette's family use him as a status symbol for, as an Englishman, he might restore Antoinette to the identity and stability of the dominant order. Both matches are initially materialistic and in both novels, the wedding is reported to have taken place in Spanish Town against a background of underhand scheming, the estranged groom being presented as an easy prey both in *Jane Eyre* and *Wide Sargasso Sea*. In both texts, the discovery of the mother's madness and of Antoinette's younger brother's illness is only made afterwards, and in both texts, Antoinette–Bertha's breathtaking beauty is felt to have been instrumental in foul play. The facts of Rochester's life, once afflicted with a mad wife, are more or less identical. Whether in Part Two of *Wide Sargasso Sea* or in *Jane Eyre*'s Chapter 27, Rochester complains about the lunatic's violent temper and her proneness to use bad language:

such language! – no professed harlot ever had a fouler vocabulary than she.[10]

Your *doudou* certainly know some filthy language. (*WSS*, 128)

The stigmas of madness are described in similar terms, although slightly more hyperbolic ones in *Jane Eyre*:

It was a discoloured face – it was a savage face. I wish I could forget the roll of the red eyes and the fearful blackened inflation of the lineaments! (*Jane Eyre*, 311)

Her hair hung uncombed and dull into her eyes which were inflamed and staring, her face was very flushed and looked swollen. (*WSS*, 120)

At times, Jean Rhys's writing almost becomes plagiaristic, against her will, as one of her letters attests: '[o]ne stupid thing I did was to read "Jane Eyre" too much. Then I found it was creeping into my writing.'[11]

Thus the influence of Charlotte Brontë's text can be traced in Jean Rhys's use of certain words. The verb 'to bewitch' is a case in point in so far as it at once indicates the plagiaristic impulse and how Jean Rhys controls it. It seems that the more Charlotte Brontë's writing 'creeps into' Jean Rhys's, the more the latter becomes creative. In *Jane Eyre*, the verb describes the way in which Rochester helplessly fell in love with plain Jane, that 'fairy [...] come from Elf-land', as he calls her (*Jane Eyre*, 296). The lexical field of fairytale partakes of the novel's romantic component. In *Wide Sargasso Sea*, the word refers to Antoinette's beauty and the evil power attached to it. Jean Rhys repeats the verb with variations: while it is used as a metaphor in *Jane Eyre*, it is literalized in the West Indian context of *Wide Sargasso Sea* where magic is common practice, and true enough, Antoinette literally tries to bewitch her husband with a love potion, which unfortunately does not fulfil her hopes. By no means, then, is repetition to be held as fruitless, plagiaristic imitation. Another passage confirms that the more precise the borrowing is, the more Jean Rhys smuggles some of her own enunciation into the original. In the following lines, Antoinette reports what her husband said to her 'off-stage':

> I took the red dress down and put it against myself. 'Does it make me look intemperate and unchaste?' I said. That man told me so. [. . .] 'Infamous daughter of an infamous mother', he said to me. (*WSS*, 152)

This is indeed a verbatim quotation from *Jane Eyre*: 'Bertha, the true daughter of an infamous mother, dragged me through all the hideous and degrading agonies which must attend a man bound to a wife at once intemperate and unchaste' (*Jane Eyre*, 334). Quoting from rather than simply echoing *Jane Eyre*, Jean Rhys distances herself from the earlier text. If the quotation marks acknowledge indebtedness, the borrowed utterance is made to feature as an interrogative clause, by which Antoinette seems to call the matrix text into question and by which *Wide Sargasso Sea* claims independence. The paradoxical co-presence of acknowledged connection and separation is most apparent in the final part where the two texts cohabit the same space, Thornfield Hall, with the cell where Antoinette–Bertha is incarcerated, the adjoining room where tapestries are hung, the lower floors into which she sneaks whenever Grace Poole's watchfulness is slackened by intoxication. *Jane Eyre* suffuses the whole of Part Three and yet, as we shall see through the analysis of the third occurrence of Antoinette's dream, this is where 'the Emancipation Act' is passed and implemented.

'The Emancipation Act'

In the opening lines, mention is made of the 'Emancipation Act' which promulgated the abolition of slavery in the British colonies. For many planters and for Antoinette's slave-owning family, Emancipation has deleterious consequences. Bringing about the end of the already economically depressed plantation system, it initiates a destructive chain reaction which does not spare Coulibri, the family's estate. Emancipation for some means bondage for others, for it leaves Antoinette's widowed mother with no status at all: belonging neither to the black community nor, as an impoverished *béké*, to the dominant class, she is trapped in isolation and comes to depend on her second husband, Mr Mason, an Englishman who, remaining blind to post-slavery racial antagonisms, will prove unable to prevent the burning of Coulibri, Antoinette's brother's death and his wife's slow descent into madness. Emancipation, therefore, also has a hand in the arrangement which, in the long run, will make Antoinette slave to her husband.

If the heroine's family does not benefit from the Emancipation Act, the text does, metaphorically declaring its emancipation from repetition. The reference to Emancipation can be interpreted as the incipient sign that with *Wide Sargasso Sea* Jean Rhys overcomes what Harold Bloom has called the 'anxiety of influence'. The dynamic of literary history, he argues, arises from this 'anxiety of influence', that is, the artist's fear that his predecessors might have exhausted all the possibilities of writing original texts. Drawing upon Freud's family romance, Harold Bloom sees the relation of the later author to his 'precursor' as one of son to father, the son engaging in Oedipal warfare with his father. Bent on asserting his own creative autonomy, the son symbolically has to kill the father, which he does by unconsciously distorting his work: 'strong poets make [poetic] history by misreading one another, so as to clear imaginative space for themselves'.[12] Thus, Harold Bloom argues, every poem is a misinterpretation of a parent poem, a misreading or 'misprision' by which the later artist tries to assert his 'priority' over earlier writings. Through his misreading of the precursor's work, which is a defence mechanism, the later poet deviates from the earlier one, and literary history emerges as a succession of deviations, of 'revisionary swerves' away from artistic father-figures.

Sandra Gilbert and Susan Gubar question the validity of Harold Bloom's distinctly male and patriarchal model which allows the feminine only the role of the muse, on the grounds that, where women writers are concerned, a tradition still remains to be created or, more accurately, is still in the making: '[t]he son of many fathers, today's male writer feels hopelessly belated; the daughter of too few mothers, today's female writer feels that she is helping to create a viable tradition which is at last definitively emerging'.[13] For Harold Bloom's 'anxiety of influence', Sandra Gilbert and Susan Gubar substitute an 'anxiety of authorship', the woman writer's 'fear that she cannot create, that because she can never become a "precursor" the act of writing will isolate or destroy her'.[14] Because creativity is defined as male, the female writer's battle 'is not against her (male) precursor's reading of the world but against his reading of *her*'. As a consequence, she tends to seek actively 'a *female* precursor who, far from representing a threatening force to be denied or killed, proves by example that a revolt against patriarchal literary authority is possible'.[15] Bearing these apt reservations in mind, I shall nonetheless turn to one of the six 'revisionary movements' Harold Bloom identifies in *The Anxiety of Influence*, for his model will prove helpful in defining the kind of emancipatory revision that Jean Rhys undertakes of her 'foremother's' work. By acknowledging indebtedness to another woman writer, she may seek to inscribe her belonging to a female literary tradition or her contribution to the emergence of such tradition, but she also inscribes her difference: she swerves away from the reading of woman that is reflected in *Jane Eyre*, in such a radical way that she makes *Wide Sargasso Sea* appear as an unprecedently original work.

One of the distorting processes which operate in reading and rewriting a 'precursor's' work is what Harold Bloom calls

> *[a]pophrades*, or the return of the dead; I take the word from the Athenian dismal or unlucky days upon which the dead returned to reinhabit the houses in which they had lived. The later poet, in his own final phase, already burdened by an imaginative solitude that is almost a solipsism, holds his own poem so open again to the precursor's work that at first we might believe the wheel has come full circle, and that we are back in the later poet's flooded apprenticeship, before his strength began to assert itself in the revisionary ratios. But the poem is now *held* open to the precursor, where once it *was* open, and the uncanny effect is that the new poem's achievement makes it seem to us, not as though the precursor were writing it, but as though the later poet himself had written the precursor's characteristic work.[16]

In effect, *Wide Sargasso Sea* is 'held open' to *Jane Eyre* but creates the illusion that it precedes the 'mother-poem' in time, 'so that the tyranny of time almost is overturned, and one can believe, for startled moments, that [it is] being *imitated by [its] ancestor*'.[17] In *Wide Sargasso Sea*, 'the mighty dead return', but Jean Rhys is the one who consciously makes them return so that they return in her colours, and speaking in her own voice. She reverses the *apophrades*, sublimating anxiety-inducing repetition into the assertion of her own priority and creativity.

The emancipation that arises from this 'revisionary ratio' is best exemplified by Antoinette's dream at the end of the novel, which in fact appears on three separate occasions. With each occurrence, more details are provided until she is allowed to seize the full significance of her dream, which has been haunting her ever since childhood. This threefold nightmare partakes of the prophetic dimension of *Wide Sargasso Sea*, although the first 'draft' is as yet only a rather sketchy prophecy: Antoinette is walking through a forest and senses that she is being followed by an unidentified person who hates her (*WSS*, 23). When the dream occurs for the second time, at the end of the first part as Antoinette is about to leave convent school (*WSS*, 50), it becomes more clearly premonitory: wearing a long, white dress, she is following a man through a forest to an enclosed garden where 'the trees are different trees'. She is terrified but cannot help following him, driven as she is by a sense of inevitability: '[t]his must happen', she says, and it is to happen at the top of a flight of stairs. At this point, it is still unclear what the pronoun 'it' refers to, but the reader has an inkling of the man's identity and the setting presages England and the place of Antoinette's confinement. Some time later, she proves to have had an even clearer vision of the house: 'I know that house where I will be cold and not belonging, the bed

I shall lie in has red curtains' (*WSS*, 92). The second occurrence of her dream prophesies her marriage with 'Rochester' and the tragic outcome of the arrangement, establishing Part Two as a rewriting of the oneiric text. If, at this stage, the dream achieves prophetic status only through a process of inference on the reader's part, the ultimate version is an overt incursion into Charlotte Brontë's fictional universe. Antoinette repeats what Bertha is reported to have done in the innkeeper's account of the final conflagration in *Jane Eyre* (Chapter 26). In her dream, Antoinette steals out of her attic rooms, ventures into the main part of the house, sets fire to it and takes shelter on the roof from which she jumps, waking up, however, before she reaches the ground. Enacting *Wide Sargasso Sea*'s final convergence with *Jane Eyre*, the dream appears as the site of the ultimate return of 'le revenant', which, as it turns out, Antoinette actually *sees*: '[i]t was then that I saw her – the ghost. The woman with streaming hair' (*WSS*, 154). One would indeed be tempted to say that, here, Antoinette eventually comes to coincide with Bertha, the image of 'streaming hair', also present in *Jane Eyre*,[18] serving as a point of identification. However, it seems to me that in Antoinette's wording, Bertha remains distinct from her, thereby signifying that Antoinette's dream is not to be taken as plain repetition.

The most important difference is that, in Antoinette's oneiric scenario, death is skilfully ruled out. For the macabre vision of Bertha's dismembered body on the pavement of Thornfield Hall – 'and then, ma'am, she yelled and gave a spring, and the next minute she lay smashed on the pavement' (*Jane Eyre*, 453) – Jean Rhys substitutes a more positive image of flight: unlike Bertha, Antoinette does not leap to her death; she jumps and returns to wakefulness before the crash. This ending is in keeping with the wish Jean Rhys expresses

in her letters: '[h]er end – I want it in a way trium-
phant!'[19] And so it is, in the sense, to start with, that
Antoinette dies neither in her dream nor in the 'reality'
of the diegesis; in the sense too that the dream at large
enacts the reversal of *apophrades* described by Harold
Bloom. This reversal is carried out through the erosion
of the limit between before and after. In her dream,
Antoinette rehearses her taking flight from the roof of
Thornfield Hall, a potentially lethal leap which will only
be actualized in *Jane Eyre*. At first sounding like the
repetition of a previous text, Antoinette's dream in fact
provides a draft version for a course of action that still
remains to be taken, so that *Jane Eyre* is made to appear
as the continuation of *Wide Sargasso Sea*, and Jean Rhys
as Charlotte Brontë's 'precursor'. Antoinette's dream is
then a prophecy of what will take place in *Jane Eyre*: only
in Charlotte Brontë's novel will Bertha–Antoinette meet
her death. Through this reversal, Jean Rhys usurps
precedence, making it seem to us as if *Wide Sargasso Sea*
came first and originated *Jane Eyre*.

Intertextuality in Jean Rhys's last novel greatly differs
from that of *Good Morning Midnight*, in which the intertextual game is a figure for exhaustion and alienation.
In *Wide Sargasso Sea*, it paradoxically represents Jean
Rhys's fantasy of unprecedented creation and helps her
overcome her 'anxiety of influence' as well as her
'anxiety of authorship'. Antoinette is no parroting
double but a kind of Cassandra, and it is now up to
Jane Eyre's Bertha to feel haunted. This transferred
feeling of hauntedness is conveyed by a repeated
question, '*Qui est là? Qui est là?*' (*WSS*, 155), which
happens to be all that the family's parrot was ever able to
articulate. That the parrot should reappear at this point
of the text – Antoinette's last dream – is of course no
accident. Coco, for such is his name, had clipped wings,
a very bad temper, limited speaking skills and, more

importantly, was killed in the burning of Coulibri. Killing this emblem of barren psittacism, the text stages its victory over repetition. On a more literal level, the death of the parrot, however traumatic, is to some extent emancipatory for Antoinette's family. Considered unlucky in West Indian superstition, the sight of the burning parrot makes the awestruck mob of the Masons' aggressors back away, which is how the latter can reach safety. In the dream's final metaphor, the mutilated bird is transfigured into a kind of phoenix rising from its ashes, a figure for creative impulse: 'the wind caught my hair and it streamed out like wings' (*WSS*, 155).

The novel at large contributes to this usurpation of precedence over *Jane Eyre*. It characteristically concentrates on the past of Charlotte Brontë's characters and the period prior to Antoinette's confinement. The events reported in Jean Rhys's novel are therefore invested with an explanatory function accounting for the couple's tragic fate. *Wide Sargasso Sea* logically assumes priority in that it builds up the causal connections from which the plot of *Jane Eyre* appears to be proceeding. This reconstruction of causality is indeed the stated motive for Jean Rhys's revision of *Jane Eyre*:

> She [the Creole] must be plausible at least with a past, the *reason* why Mr Rochester treats her abominably and feels justified, the *reason* why he thinks she is mad and why of course she goes mad, even the *reason* why she tries to set everything on fire, and eventually succeeds.[20]

Seeking to explain 'the why and the wherefore'[21] of Antoinette's madness, Jean Rhys appropriates the genesis of Bertha. In doing so, she also implies that she is willing to correct what she deems to be defective characterization, overtly criticizing the 'precursor' for her treatment of the character of the mad wife who, Jean Rhys complains, is no more than a 'paper tiger lunatic'[22] in *Jane Eyre*. She accordingly undertakes to flesh her out into a more fully rounded whole. In Charlotte Brontë's novel, the account of Bertha's life is quickly disposed of in one single chapter (Chapter 27), in which she essentially features as a by-product of Victorian ideology, her madness typically resulting from excess.[23] Until then, her substance is limited to that of 'a horrible laughter', or of a 'shape' reminiscent of 'the foul German spectre – the vampire' (*Jane Eyre*, 311). Only once is she allowed to go on to the diegetic stage and when she is, she appears as a hybrid creature, a composite of woman and beast:

> In the deep shade, at the farther end of the room, a figure ran backwards and forwards. What it was, whether beast or human being, one could not, at first sight tell: it grovelled, seemingly, on all fours; it snatched and growled like some strange wild animal: but it was covered with clothing, and a quantity of dark, grizzled hair, wild as a mane, hid its head and face. (*Jane Eyre*, 321)

Jean Rhys replaces the pronoun 'it' which so often refers to Bertha in *Jane Eyre*[24] with a more human 'she' and even with an 'I', since she promotes the grovelling creature, producing what Jane calls 'oral oddities' (*Jane Eyre*, 142), to the status of a speaking subject. Gaining access to articulate speech, Antoinette–Bertha is freed from the strictures of the stereotype, which leads Michael Thorpe to define Jean Rhys's revision as 'an act of moral restitution to the stereotyped lunatic heiress in Rochester's attic'.[25]

Jane Eyre: A Wintry Romance

'There is always the other side, always', Antoinette says to her husband as she tries to persuade him that Daniel Cosway's assertions are slanderous (*WSS*, 106). In her revision of *Jane Eyre*, Jean Rhys bends all her imaginative powers towards producing such relativizing: she writes about and from 'the other side', creating an alternative version to Rochester's account of his first marriage in *Jane Eyre*. She actually reverses the perspective, as one of her letters attests:

> The Creole in Charlotte Brontë's novel is a lay figure – repulsive which does not matter, and not once alive which does. She's necessary to the plot, but always she shrieks, howls and laughs horribly, attacks all and sundry – *off stage*. For me (and for you I hope) she must be right *on stage*.[26]

What is off-stage, behind the scenes in *Jane Eyre*, Jean Rhys places centre-stage in *Wide Sargasso Sea*. Reversing the perspective, she also tends to reverse the significance of Jane's autobiography, which could be defined as a chronicle of suppression. Donald D. Stone, for instance, describes Charlotte Brontë's novel as follows: '[a] Victorianized romance celebrating the virtues of home and duty is the reward for the rejection of the excesses of romance and Romanticism'.[27] Reworking this celebration of restraint and self-control – this is by no means the only possible reading of *Jane Eyre* – Jean Rhys liberates all that *Jane Eyre* represses. In her search for an alternative idiom, she elaborates precisely those elements which Charlotte Brontë suppresses, especially those having to do with romance.

It is undeniable that *Jane Eyre* borrows from the conventional material of romance, the marriage plot in particular: Jane, the plain servant in whom many have seen a Victorian Cinderella, will against all odds marry her upper-class master. Her 'pilgrim's progress' is structured along the lines of traditional quest–romance which, as Northrop Frye points out, is a dialectical form, focused as it is on a conflict between the hero and his enemy.[28] Jane is accordingly put to the test: on the way to wish-fulfilment, she has to confront various obstacles and impediments, including her own demons, which are the modern avatars of the canonical dragon the hero must overcome in romance. Thornfield Hall is the site of Jane's crucial struggle, after which, all tensions being resolved, the 'thorns' are removed, together with the raging monster which had been haunting the premises. In due course, for the romantic quest is a successful one, the little governess and her beloved master are reunited and they live happily ever after, at Ferndean, a cross between 'the enclosed bower' and 'the pleasure dome',[29] where Jane is rewarded with the mild comforts of the domestic hearth after the agony of devilish conflagration.

There has been much debate over the nature of Jane's struggle. For some, wish-fulfilment is attained at the cost of sacrifice. If the orphan shepherdess eventually marries the prince of love, she does so at a price. First, the prince she marries is a decidedly froglike one, a considerably impaired Byronic hero. Moreover, this mitigated achievement has required much personal renunciation. She has had to subdue her fiery temper and romantic turmoil, to follow the dictates of reason and to learn a lesson of moderation. For Pauline Nestor, for example, 'Jane's survival depends on her ability to mediate between the potentially destructive extremes of her own character – between the poles of Reason and Feeling, "absolute submission and determined revolt".'[30] For others, *Jane Eyre* is neither about renunciation nor compromise. Refusing the either/or antinomy, love/ independence, Jane embarks on an uncompromising journey towards selfhood, implying escape from the thrall of dependence. Hers is a passionate quest for liberty and autonomy and her reward, Michelle A. Massé argues, is 'a new world in which love and women's identities need not be contradictions, where men and women can meet, as Jane once proclaimed, as "equals" '.[31]

Whatever the interpretation, and although Charlotte Brontë borrows from romance, it is equally undeniable that she distances herself from the conventions of the genre and the ideology that underlies them, refuting the romantic notion that 'any woman can be swept in good Cinderella fashion from obscurity into the loving embrace of the man in whom she'll find her world'.[32] Sandra Gilbert and Susan Gubar, for example, underscore the 'rebellious feminism' of this *realistic* romance which challenges the forms, customs and standards of society. For them, Jane is a woman 'who yearns to escape entirely from drawing-rooms and patriarchal mansions'.[33] Charlotte Brontë may borrow from drawing-room literature, but she also ironically disqualifies its formulae, so that traditional romance, the 'mythos of summer' in Northrop Frye's terms, is tempered and chilled by irony, the 'mythos of winter'.[34] A wintry romance, *Jane Eyre* suppresses the romantic impulse by ironically disparaging the fairytale motifs from which romance is derived. This is particularly true of the first meeting between Jane and Rochester. It is, on the face of it, a fairytale encounter: at dusk, in the icy cold, lonely countryside, Jane spots a rider on a 'tall steed', preceded by 'a lion-like dog' which reminds Jane of 'a North-of-England spirit, called a "Gytrash"' (*Jane Eyre*, 143). The scene is set for romance but the next minute, rider and steed lie flat on the ice and only the dog comes up to Jane's romantic expectations; as she ironically notes, '[t]he man, the human being, broke the spell at once' (*Jane Eyre*, 144). Charlotte Brontë clearly curtails the fairytale element through literally damaging irony, for it is the same irony that maims and blinds Rochester at the end of the novel.

Gothic romance is likewise suppressed, a suppression which, according to Michelle A. Massé, is suggestive of Jane's refusal of the Gothic beating fantasy.[35] The mechanisms of the Gothic are undercut with an infusion of what Robert B. Heilman calls 'the anti-Gothic'.[36] In one of the most famous passages where Jane first hears Bertha's demoniac laugh, Gothic imagination is aroused, only to be frustrated by the appearance of Grace Poole, whom Jane mistakes for the woman who laughed in so eerie a fashion: 'any apparition less romantic or less ghostly could scarcely be conceived' (*Jane Eyre*, 138). Grace Poole acts 'as a damper' to the Gothic (*Jane Eyre*, 142), and so do Jane's intrusions as narrator. Of course, Jane is wrong when she thinks that what she heard was earthy Grace's laugh, but what she witnessed is no ghostly manifestation either; it is the laughter of all too real a woman. In the sequence where Bertha sets fire to Rochester's bed, initially presented as 'a marrow-freezing incident' (*Jane Eyre*, 179), comedy serves as another 'palliative of straight Gothic'.[37] Jane flies to her master's assistance and Gothic terror is indeed defused when Rochester, soaking wet, wakes up 'fulminating strange anathemas at finding himself lying in a pool of water' (*Jane Eyre*, 180). More importantly, Gothic is annulled through metaphorical displacement. In *Jane Eyre*, uncanny manifestations are primarily symptoms of inner conflicts threatening the self with dissolution. The first case of hauntedness occurs in the red-room at Gateshead where, as a child, Jane is locked up after a rebellious fit. The red-room is clearly a Gothic *topos*: stately and remote, it is the death chamber where Mr Reed breathed his last. The text paves the way for 'some coming vision from another world' (*Jane Eyre*, 49), but thanks to the narrating 'I's' immediate provision of a rational explanation – 'I can now conjecture readily that this streak of light was, in all likelihood, a gleam from a lanterna carried by some one across the lawn' (*Jane Eyre*, 49) – it redirects attention towards a psychological reading of the uncanny. A creation of Jane's fevered mind, brought about by rage, the Gothic phenomenon reads as a metaphor for the romantic excesses she must channel. In the same way, Bertha, the main prop of the Gothic at Thornfield Hall, is no other than Jane's dark double, an 'objective correlative' of the pitfalls from which she must learn to stay clear. As Donald D. Stone puts it, 'Bertha represents, to be sure, Romantic energy at its most willful and uncontrolled, *la bête humaine* personified.'[38] Sandra Gilbert and Susan Gubar see her as 'Jane's truest and darkest double: she is the angry aspect of the orphan child, the ferocious secret self Jane has been trying to repress ever since childhood'.[39] Jane's affinities with Bertha check any inclination we may have to see the 'spectre' as a truly Gothic creature. Charlotte Brontë calls for an allegorical reading of the Gothic *topoi*. Such a reading, Tzvetan Todorov has shown, is incompatible with fantasy.[40] When it is 'naturalized' as allegory or symbolism, fantasy loses its proper non-signifying nature, its fundamental capacity to induce hesitation, its resistance to closed meaning and interpretation.

Wide Sargasso Sea: A Tropical Romance

Where Charlotte Brontë tempers the romantic element in an attempt to present the reader with a realistically drawn woman, Jane, who is seen to outgrow and reject the restricting formulae of traditional romance, Jean Rhys, by contrast, seems to seek in romance new options for the feminine. Taking the opposite course to Charlotte

Brontë's domesticated quest–romance, Jean Rhys turns to a more canonical form, stripped, that is, of the wintry attire of irony. *Wide Sargasso Sea*, as she says in one of her letters, is a 'romantic novel (my first Romance)'.[41] Reversing Charlotte Brontë's 'romance of reality' into 'a romantic novel', she incorporates into the novel elements that escape patriarchal taxonomies, while restoring romance to the summery clime to which it belongs, to the heat, even, of subtropical, unending 'summer'. Displacing Charlotte Brontë's cast of characters to the West Indies, Jean Rhys mobilizes the archetypes of the genre, so much so that *Wide Sargasso Sea* could be defined as an 'archi-romance', at once a more archaic form of romance and a romance of extremity.

The setting in *Wide Sargasso Sea* is typical of romantic topography. If, in *Jane Eyre*, the West Indies are an overheated, madness-inducing milieu, they are presented as an idyllic, ideal world in *Wide Sargasso Sea*, a modern Eden that is not unlike the type of setting that serves as a backdrop for today's cheap romances. Yet, as the description of Coulibri suggests, the garden of Eden is also a fallen one:

> Our garden was large and beautiful as that garden in the Bible – the tree of life grew there. But it had gone wild. The paths were overgrown and a smell of dead flowers mixed with the fresh living smell. (*WSS*, 16–17)

As well as invoking 'the past and the socially remote' as romantic settings tend to do,[42] nineteenth-century Jamaica and Dominica bear the marks of the conventional *agon* or conflict between an 'idyllic world' and a 'demonic or night world' in Northrop Frye's terms. The 'powerful polarizing tendency'[43] of romance structures the universe of Granbois in particular: it is a dream-place, remote, almost out of reach, whose 'intoxicating

freshness' and 'untouched' quality 'Rochester' underlines on several occasions (*WSS*, 61, 73). As the site of the
couple's honeymoon, Granbois corresponds to the
romantic universe of wish-fulfilment and of unrest-
rained sexual fulfilment – 'In sunlight, in shadow, by
moonlight, by candlelight' (*WSS*, 77) – but it is not long
before 'Rochester' senses a malevolent presence that
might at any moment carry him from the idyllic to the
demonic. Fallen Granbois does not go without its snakes
or its Leviathan, the 'monster crab' that lurks under a
flat stone in the river (*WSS*, 73).

In spite of the reference to the Bible, the code of good
and evil in *Wide Sargasso Sea* and in romance in general
'is formulated in a magical, rather than a purely ethical,
sense' as Fredric Jameson puts it.[44] The polarity of the
universe of *Wide Sargasso Sea* is an archaic, magical one,
giving pride of place to a primitive animism in which
things and places are granted human feelings and
powers. Granbois alternately is a hostile, menacing
presence for 'Rochester' or a friendly, benevolent one
for Antoinette. This is not to be read as pathetic fallacy;
Granbois is 'really' ambivalent. 'Rochester' will be
bewitched by its literally spellbinding charm *and* its
baleful powers. In this magical world, Christophine, an
obeah woman, plays a prominent role. If the text never
directly stages any of her occult activities and although
obeah is, it seems, taboo as well as illegal, it nonetheless
suffuses the text, in much the same way as Bertha's
hidden presence suffuses the plot of *Jane Eyre*. Unlike
Bertha, however, obeah is not a metaphor. The love
potion which Christophine concocts for Antoinette
provides a fair illustration of its literality and, inciden-
tally, of the unsensational way in which magic is dealt
with. The reader is not made privy to the actual making
of the potion and all we are allowed to see is Antoinette
leaving Christophine with something 'wrapped in a leaf'

(*WSS*, 98). Moreover, whatever it is that Christophine has given her seems to be denied any magical efficacy; it barely makes 'Rochester' very sick and fails to counteract the gradual dereliction of the couple's relationship. The love potion does not work and yet it does in a way. Far from being ineffective, the presumably magical potion acts upon reality. Believing that he is being poisoned, 'Rochester' is at this precise point overwhelmed by rage and hatred, and 'miraculously' assumes the identity of the Satanic victimizer. What is more, his metamorphosis, in which the love potion definitely has a hand, proves to be the all too predictable enactment of Christophine's prophetic warnings: '[t]oo besides, [obeah] is not for *béké*. Bad, bad trouble come when *béké* meddle with that' (*WSS*, 93). In this understated way, the text establishes Christophine as a magician and a prophetess, and designates itself as a magical narrative or a magic formula effecting the merger of archaic romance and realistic mode. If magic is realistically motivated by the West Indian context, it is not suppressed in the name of realism as romance is in *Jane Eyre*.

Suppression is by no means on the agenda of *Wide Sargasso Sea*. Contrary to *Jane Eyre*, it articulates an aesthetic of extremity, while meeting the demands of plausibility. The novel's treatment of causality is emblematic of the nuptials of romantic and mimetic modes. *Wide Sargasso Sea* was born out of a wish to motivate the character of Bertha. Retracing the genesis of her madness, Jean Rhys undertakes to emancipate Bertha from the debilitating straitjacket of stereotyped and non-plausible characterization. This motivating causality, however, is itself brought to an extreme. To all the rational motives accounting for Antoinette's madness and subsequent incarceration, Jean Rhys adds less rational ones in a prophetic narrative where, as we have seen, things seem to happen *because* they were predicted. Such causal strategy is a subversion of verisimilitude which depends on what Gérard Genette calls a 'causalistic alibi', by which the plausible narrative seeks to conceal the fundamentally arbitrary nature of fiction.[45] Ascribing a cause to everything, including when the cause is non-rational, is an exaggeration and a violation of the grammar of plausible motivation, and calls to mind the 'pan-determinism' of the fantastic. The concept, which was coined by Tzvetan Todorov,[46] refers to fantasy's dislike of chance, that is, causal void, a dislike which prompts fantastic narratives to call upon supernatural causes in preference to deficient causality.

In *Wide Sargasso Sea*, lacks are indeed systematically filled and excess is recommended where *Jane Eyre* advocates temperance and self-control. Excess is 'naturally' indigenous to the universe of *Wide Sargasso Sea*, as strangers like Mr Mason or 'Rochester' repeatedly note: '[a]lways one extreme or the other', Mason says of Antoinette's mother (*WSS*, 28). Like mother, like daughter: excess is inscribed in Antoinette's body – 'her eyes [. . .] are too large and can be disconcerting' (*WSS*, 56). On his way to Granbois, the true seat of extremity, 'Rochester' is dumbfounded by the daunting intensity of the surroundings:

> Everything is too much, I felt as I rode wearily after her. Too much blue, too much purple, too much green. The flowers too red, the mountains too high, the hills too near. (*WSS*, 59)

The silence is 'absolute' (*WSS*, 86), the noise 'deafening' and the moths are the size of birds (*WSS*, 68). 'Rochester's' wish to put a check on excess is actually what will cause tragedy to prevail over the idyllic world of romance.

Jean Rhys gives free rein to everything that is suppressed in *Jane Eyre*. In the same way as she takes excess 'out of the closet' and generally makes manifest what is hidden in *Jane Eyre*, she removes Gothic fantasy from the strictures of the subtext in which it is confined in *Jane Eyre*. This she does in her customary economical way, for she does not resort to what Anthony Luengo calls 'the traditional claptrap' of the Gothic.[47] The fact nonetheless remains, he argues, that the true literary context of *Wide Sargasso Sea* is the Gothic mode of fiction. Anthony Luengo convincingly lists a number of typically Gothic devices and motifs, tracing Jean Rhys's indebtedness to Gothic fiction to the 'subjective nature of landscape description',[48] among other things. The menacing forest surrounding Granbois reflects 'Rochester's' increasing anguish and plays the same role in *Wide Sargasso Sea* as it does in American Gothic where, for obvious reasons, it has come to serve as a substitute for the gloomy medieval castles of European Gothic. In the Gothic of *Wide Sargasso Sea*, nature has taken the place of architecture.

Another typically Gothic feature is the presence of ruins. For Anthony Luengo, the ruins which 'Rochester' comes upon in the tropical forest signify a defunct 'feudal order', the defunct plantation system, and connote 'a Radcliffean or romantic apprehension of mutability'.[49] Magic and superstition are also *topoi* of the 'terror–Gothic' of course. So are the ghosts which, according to him, should be read as mental phenomena or figures of speech – as in *Jane Eyre*. Finally, Jean Rhys revises the conventions of Gothic characterization by conflating different types. 'Rochester' starts as a romantic suitor and quickly turns into the Gothic villain, while Antoinette is at once a persecuted woman and a *femme fatale*. This problematization of the simple polarities of Gothic romance, Anthony Luengo concludes, is a symptom of the crisis of identity at issue in *Wide Sargasso Sea*, which he defines as 'a novel about anxiety'.[50] It seems to me that this is an oversimplification of the significance of both *Wide Sargasso Sea* and the Gothic, and that Anthony Luengo's definition fails to pinpoint the specificity of Rhysian Gothic for, if her Gothic is the vehicle of anxiety, then Jean Rhys merely follows in Charlotte Brontë's footsteps and imitates nineteenth-century Gothic which, as Rosemary Jackson puts it, 'is progressively turned inwards to concern itself with psychological problems, used to dramatize uncertainty and conflicts of the individual subject in relation to a difficult social situation'.[51]

Fantastic Destabilization

The answer to the question of the specificity of Rhysian Gothic might emerge from a study of the interaction of the Gothic and realistic modes, a correlation which Rosemary Jackson thoroughly examines in her theory of fantasy:

> The fantastic exists as the inside, or underside, of realism, opposing the novel's closed, monological forms with open, dialogical structures, as if the novel had given rise to its own opposite, its unrecognizable reflection.[52]

As the other of realism, fantasy challenges it with 'open structures'. In Jean Rhys's practice, the dialogue between fantasy and plausibility is exacerbated in order to subvert the patriarchal categorization of the real and also to palliate what consensual taxonomies fail to apprehend: it gives utterance to all that is not said, to all that is unsayable within the dominant order, to all that it registers only as absence. Symptomatically, Antoinette's mother belongs to those 'areas which can be conceptualized only by negative terms'.[53] Contrary to Mr Mason, who is 'so without a doubt English', Annette is 'so without a doubt not English, but no white nigger either' (*WSS*, 30). If there is a signifier for Mr Mason, there is none for Annette, who is clearly unnameable. In Part Two, right from the start of his narrative, the male narrator himself acknowledges the loopholes in the dominant idiom: '[a]s for my confused impressions they will never be written. There are blanks in my mind that cannot be filled up' (*WSS*, 64). *Wide Sargasso Sea* systematically exposes the faulty grasp of discourse on a disorienting reality, concentrating on what Rosemary Jackson, after Samuel Beckett, calls 'nameless things' and 'thingless names'.[54] Hence the mystery 'Rochester' feels in his new surroundings, the sense of a hidden thing, of a secret that is being kept from his groping mind (*WSS*, 73). Like any fantastic text, *Wide Sargasso Sea* creates 'epistemological uncertainty',[55] uncertainty of vision and interpretation, resisting fixity and stable identifications.

Reluctant to present any definitive version of an ultimate truth, it resorts to narrative instability, central to the fantastic. The gap between signifier and signified, which is typical of the fantastic as a 'literature of separation',[56] is left open by the text's multi-voicedness. Conflicting views and interpretations are made to cohabit in endless dialogue and unsolvable equivocation. Signs are vulnerable to multiple and contradictory interpretation and no omniscient, authoritative voice comes to restore the reader to certainty. If uncertainty is derived from the inscription of double views, each narrator also proves to be intrinsically unreliable. Antoinette, whose vision we might be tempted to trust, is said to be 'undecided, uncertain about facts – any fact'

(*WSS*, 73). The other contradictory visions, which we are inclined to distrust, prove to hold an element of truth. Such is the case when both Daniel Cosway and Amélie suggest that Antoinette is having an affair with Sandi, her lifelong friend (*WSS*, 100, 103). As nothing, either in Antoinette's narrative or 'Rochester's', substantiates the assertion, this sounds like yet another infamous accusation. Yet, in Part Three, as Antoinette takes over the narrating, Sandi's name crops up again, confirming in retrospect that Antoinette has really had an adulterous *liaison* with him (*WSS*, 152) and consequently casting retroactive doubt on her reliability. In such narrative economy, the truth, 'Rochester' complains, cannot but recede further and further into the distance: '[h]ow can one discover truth I thought and that thought led me nowhere' (*WSS*, 86). This is particularly true of the most Gothic episode in *Wide Sargasso Sea*, the sequence among the ruins which he discovers in the forest. First, perception becomes increasingly confused as 'Rochester' is seized by hallucination: he has the feeling that somebody is watching him but the place is deserted (*WSS*, 86). Then he comes upon the vestiges of a paved road whose existence will be categorically denied by Baptiste, the servant (*WSS*, 87). It seems that the line between what is and what is not can no longer be drawn in a world where certainties dissolve and where, as a result, 'Rochester' can only lose his bearings – he gets lost in the forest. Finally, uncertainty destabilizes his own identity, as a little girl runs away in a fright, having taken him for a zombi, in other words, a compound of life and death which defies rational categorization.

The impulse behind this opening activity or disjunction of word and meaning is a wish for novelty: Jean Rhys seeks to invest words with a new signifying power. Through the import of fantasy, she invents fresh possibilities for language, 'recreates and reshapes language', in Helen Carr's words, 'to map the unknown and uncharted world of ambivalence'.[57] As a 'literature of separation', the fantastic undermines predictable relations between signifier and signified but it does so, at least in Jean Rhys's practice, in order to construct new, unexpected signifying combinations and to articulate the unnameable. To this end, *Wide Sargasso Sea* engages in 'a dissolution of separating categories',[58] mainly through the agency of two figures, simile and oxymoron.

The Text's Madness

Rosemary Jackson claims that simile is incompatible with the fantastic: 'the fantastic does not proceed by analogy – it is not based upon simile and comparison (like, as, as if) but upon equation (this *did* happen)'.[59] In this, she agrees with Tzvetan Todorov's idea that the fantastic effect often proceeds from the literalization of a figure of speech. In *Wide Sargasso Sea*, however, the fantastic effect is paradoxically engineered by simile. Thanks to simile, Jean Rhys gives *explicit* utterance to things which cannot be articulated in the dominant idiom and are relegated to a silent subtext. Thus simile partakes of a movement towards completion – *Wide Sargasso Sea* completes, makes manifest the subtext of *Jane Eyre* – which could be seen as another form of romantic wish-fulfilment. A simile explicitly tells us what a metaphor merely nudges us into noting. It does not mean anything but what lies on the surface of the words, used in their literal sense. This is not to suggest that simile does not say more than each of the paired terms; the comparison of one thing to another opens up new inflections through which mystery, darkness and difference are charted. In the following dialogue between

Antoinette and 'Rochester', simile appears as the figure of the unknown:

> 'Is it true', she said, 'that England is like a dream? ...'
> 'Well', I answered annoyed, 'that is precisely how your beautiful island seems to me, quite unreal and like a dream'. (*WSS*, 67)

In this particular sequence, Antoinette's simile does not shed much light on the nature of the compared term, 'England'; on the contrary, it tends to cloud its finite identity. Far from contributing to clarification and to the closure of meaning, it problematizes identification and deconstructs familiar categories. The comparing element 'like a dream' is moreover applied to two different places, England and Antoinette's island, which makes initially separate entities come close, as if they were interchangeable. In order to 'map the unknown', the simile disfigures familiar maps. In the process, it also breaks the limit between 'fiction' (extradiegetic England) and 'reality' (the diegetic island), inviting the reader to bridge unbridgeable gaps between normally distinct levels.

Simile becomes still more frequent as 'Rochester's' reason is increasingly challenged by the island's alien logic. Once Antoinette has become the raving 'wild-haired stranger' who comprehensively curses her husband, the scene, for all its screeching 'reality', is again 'like a dream' (*WSS*, 122), so that dream and reality are almost fused, in the same way as the boundary between sleep and wakefulness is overlapped by Antoinette: 'when she wake it's as if she still sleeping', Christophine says (*WSS*, 128). At the end of Part Two, as 'Rochester' still hesitates between love and hate, reason and folly, geographical borders are no longer definite: starting

with a simile comparing the cool weather to that of an
English summer, 'Rochester' shifts to plain equation: 'it's
an English summer now, so cool, so grey' (*WSS*, 135).
The fantastic equation occurs only for a time, for it is not
long before 'Rochester' recovers his senses: the 'mad
conflicting emotions' soon subside to leave him 'sane'
(*WSS*, 141). From this point on, 'dreams are dreams'
again (*WSS*, 137) and clear-cut boundaries are restored.
However, the restoration of sanity and of rational
categorization coincides with the moment when the
male narrator's voice is silenced. Unable to withstand
the pressure of his 'conflicting emotions' and of the
dissolution of familiar categories, 'Rochester', eventually
opting for univocal and irreversible hatred, returns to
the either/or dichotomy which condemns him to silence
and denies him access to the secret of Antoinette's world,
its fundamental ambiguity and reversibility. Of course,
Antoinette knows the secret and does her utmost to
share it with him. When, for instance, she tries to
explain that he has not really been lied to about her
mother's death, she tells him that there are always 'two
deaths, the real one and the one people know about'
(*WSS*, 106). In Antoinette's subversive, feminine logic,
what is by definition unique and irreversible becomes
plural and reversible. In her wording, moreover, the
death which is registered on the death certificate is less
real than the symbolic one ('the real one').

The negation of irreversibility, which takes the shape
of an aberrant doubling in the previous sequence (two
deaths), is more often conducted through the pairing of
opposites. If few oxymorons in the strict sense of the
word are to be found in the text, many passages bring
quasi-antinomical elements together, so much so that
Wide Sargasso Sea as a whole may be described as a
realized oxymoron. This is consistent with the fantastic
which, according to Rosemary Jackson, is not so much

irrational as anti-rational, the inverse side of reason's orthodoxy:

> Contradictions surface and are held antinomically in the fantastic text, as reason is made to confront all that it traditionally refuses to encounter. The structure of fantastic narrative is one founded upon contradictions. [...] What emerges as the basic trope of fantasy is the *oxymoron*, a figure of speech which holds together contradictions and sustains them in an impossible unity, without progressing towards synthesis.[60]

As is the case with simile, oxymoron mobilizes the stated meaning of the paired terms; it is not a figure of the implicit. Through oxymoron, Jean Rhys gives explicit utterance to the mysteries which transcend patriarchal sense and logic. Conjoining two terms that in ordinary usage are contraries, oxymoron plays the game of the impossible. Its unresolvable paradox is an overt violation of what is generally accepted as possibility.

On his arrival in the West Indies, 'Rochester' is disoriented by constant irruptions of the inadmissible into what he had up to then believed to be changeless legality. Contradictions ceaselessly muddle up his perception of the world into which he has been precipitated. Inexplicably, Hilda, one of the servants, alternately wears 'a sweet childish smile' and 'giggles loudly and rudely' (*WSS*, 75). Reason or the codes of behaviour 'Rochester' is familiar with cannot help him come to terms with such abrupt changes. Like Hilda, Antoinette is an oxymoronic being. She is, in 'Rochester's' own terms, a 'lunatic who always knows the time. But never does' (*WSS*, 136). By the standards of common sense, interpretation is impossible and the only meaning that can be derived from these utterances is that Antoinette is the ultimate signifier of contradiction. 'Rochester' is caught in this oxymoronic logic and before he returns to the either/or regime and the orthodoxy of sanity, he is subject to unpredictable mutations between love and hate, desire to love and desire to harm, sudden shifts which he calls 'the giddy change' (*WSS*, 139). What makes him giddy is not so much the mere reversal of categories as the 'dissolution of separating categories':

> Desire, Hatred, Life, Death came very close in the darkness. Better not know how close. Better not think, never for a moment. Not close. The same . . . (*WSS*, 79)

Tormented by the ever-shifting quality of this universe, unable to fix things as explicable and known, he is eventually silenced, forever 'longing for what [he] had lost before [he] had found it' (*WSS*, 141). Defeated, he spitefully decides to repress and subjugate the oxymoronic creature he has married. He solves the unsolvable by appropriating it as an object: 'my lunatic. She's mad but *mine, mine*' (*WSS*, 136).

It is an object, however, which will always escape him, for Antoinette will not be silenced. She is given the last word as 'Rochester' is evicted from the narrative, and is thus able to implement the law of the oxymoron by which the male speaker has proved unable to abide. As Nancy R. Harrison puts it, 'Rhys structures her novel to show us how a muted text can be revealed to dominate a formerly "dominant" text.'[61] At the end of his narrative, 'Rochester' re-establishes the separation between opposites, between madness and sanity in particular, which is in keeping with the masculine stance, if Shoshana Felman is to be believed. She argues that madness is a label imposed upon feminine difference by 'virile reason'.[62] Jean Rhys's purpose is to strip the feminine of its masculine labelling while articulating the unsayable which the symbolic order tends to designate as madness.[63] Within the symbolic order, the feminine is, as 'Rochester's' attitude towards Antoinette exemplifies, either silent or mad. Jean Rhys circumvents this double bind by creating an 'un-mad' character who assumes the discursive positions of neither the insane nor the sane. Antoinette does not sound mad to the reader and yet cannot be deemed entirely sane. A new order of discourse emerges from the abolition of the patriarchal dichotomy sanity/madness and from the oxymoronic alliance of contraries. The end of *Wide Sargasso Sea* testifies to the fact that, between common sense and nonsense, there is room for an alternative signifying mode, another grammar which crosses the boundaries between inside and outside, subject and object, reason and madness, and yet continues to make sense.

Thus in the last part of *Wide Sargasso Sea*, space and time as we know them disintegrate. The markers Antoinette uses are unprecedented and it is only thanks to the mother-text that the reader recognizes the place where she is incarcerated. Her prison, we are told, is in a country which is not England and the house is 'made of cardboard' (*WSS*, 148). Space still makes sense, but in no way is it a commonplace space. Similarly, chronology does not mean anything to Antoinette – 'when was last night?' (*WSS*, 148) – but her red dress does make sense: reminding her of times past and of what she must do in the near future (set fire to the house), it presides over the countless time-shifts that deconstruct chronological linearity in the whole of Part Three. In this new order, time is no longer irreversible. At the end of Antoinette's dream, all the various planes collide in an unheard-of ordering. The sky provides a syncretic sum total where Antoinette's life acquires meaning:

It was red and all my life was in it. I saw the grandfather clock and Aunt Cora's patchwork, all colours, I saw the orchids and the stephanotis and the jasmine and the tree of life in flames. I saw the chandelier and the red carpet downstairs and the bamboos and the tree ferns, the gold ferns and the silver, and the soft green velvet of the moss on the garden wall. I saw my doll's house and the books and the picture of the Miller's Daughter. I heard the parrot call as he did when he saw a stranger, *Qui est là? Qui est là?* and the man who hated me calling too, Bertha! Bertha! (*WSS*, 155)

This random list of items, which comes and goes between natural and cultural elements and conflates different times and places, does not quite satisfy common sense and yet this illogical accumulation leads to an epiphany: '[n]ow I know why I was brought here and what I have to do' (*WSS*, 155). Meaning is to be found in this miscellaneous patchwork whose organizing principle is neither chronology nor even associative memory. The only connection between the various items is the conjunction 'and', which makes distinct units cohabit the same syntactic and existential plane and establishes a relationship of equality between them. This unusual accretion is akin to the functioning of oxymoron. The repetition of 'and' could be interpreted as the victory of oxymoronic impossibility over the either/or of patriarchy. In Antoinette's new grammar, two reputedly incompatible pronouns referring to the same antecedent can coexist: '[s]omeone screamed and I thought, *why did I scream?*' (*WSS*, 155). This, of course, is a violation of the grammar of identity as we know it, but this grammatical impossibility is by no means nonsensical. The speaking 'I' feels other, beside herself, and literalizes this feeling of exteriority in a third-person pronoun ('someone'), crossing the limit between subject and object and undoing gender demarcations. Recognition is no longer possible: when Richard Mason pays a visit to Antoinette, he does not recognize her (*WSS*, 151). Nor does Antoinette recognize herself, for that matter. One of the first indications about the place where she is confined is that there is no looking-glass, so that she does not know what she looks like or who she is (*WSS*, 147). Although this could easily be seen as the ultimate in alienation, it may also be an inscription of Antoinette's breaking free from the strictures of the masculine identifications of women that have been passed down through the centuries – Antoinette makes it clear that she is not Bertha either. Difference has overcome and yet, in Jean Rhys's perspective, this difference is not identified as madness.

In *Wide Sargasso Sea*, the female narrator is no longer the speaker of a muted idiom. In her reworking of Charlotte Brontë's novel, Jean Rhys unearths the hidden plot of *Jane Eyre* and gives voice to its muted subtext. In her previous works, as Nancy R. Harrison puts it, Jean Rhys presents 'a body of language, the corpse of masculine discourse as she experiences it. Into the body of the masculine idiom she inserts her own, that "unspoken" half of the dialogue.'[64] As we have seen, the 'unspoken half' may take the shape of resistance to closure, to the confining norms and categories within which women are caught. Jean Rhys wages a subterranean war against them by incorporating critical commentary into their own structures through irony or parodic mimicry. In her last novel, Jean Rhys departs from her rhetoric of the implicit. While *Voyage in the Dark* displays two conflicting idioms, one of which is muted or, being limited to Anna's silent soliloquies, runs as subtext to the main narrative, *Wide Sargasso Sea* makes the bracketed subtext surface on a

par with the masculine text. Morever, the once-
silent word prevails in the last part as Antoinette gives
loud and clear utterance to a gender-free idiom that
transcends male paradigms for female experience.
The uncharted territory into which Jean Rhys probes
through – paradoxically enough – her rewriting of *Jane
Eyre* marks the completion of the feminine quest for
(literary) self-creation.

Notes

Chapter 1: Introduction

1. Elgin W. Mellown, *Jean Rhys: A Descriptive and Annotated Bibliography of Works and Criticism* (New York: Garland Publishing Inc., 1984), p. viii. The main sources for this biographical outline are: Jean Rhys, *Letters 1931–1966* (1984; Harmondsworth: Penguin, 1985); Jean Rhys, *Smile Please* (1979; Harmondsworth: Penguin, 1981); Carole Angier, *Jean Rhys: Life and Work* (London: André Deutsch, 1990).

2. 'It was after supper that night [...] that it happened. My fingers tingled, and the palms of my hands. I pulled the chair up to the table, opened an exercise book, and wrote *This is my Diary*. But it was not a diary. I remembered everything that had happened to me in the last year and a half. I remembered what he'd said, what I'd felt. I wrote on until late into the night, till I was so tired that I couldn't go on, and I fell into bed and slept' (Rhys, *Smile Please*, p. 129).

3. Jean Rhys, *The Left Bank and Other Stories* (London: Jonathan Cape, 1927).

4. Wally Look Lai, 'The Road to Thornfield Hall: A Review of *Wide Sargasso Sea*', *New Beacon Reviews* (1968), pp. 38–52.

5. Kenneth Ramchand, *The West Indian Novel and its Background* (1970; London: Heinemann, 1983), p. 223.

6. Teresa O'Connor, *Jean Rhys: The West Indian Novels* (New York: New York University Press, 1986).

7. Quoted by Francis Wyndham in his introduction to *WSS*, p. 5.

8. Thomas F. Staley, *Jean Rhys: A Critical Study* (London: Macmillan, 1979), p. 10.

9. *Ibid.*, p. 35.

10. *Ibid.*

11. Helen Carr, *Jean Rhys* (Plymouth: Northcote House, 1996), p. 18.

12. Judith Kegan Gardiner, '*Good Morning Midnight*, Good Night Modernism', *Boundary 2*, no. 1–2, vol. 11 (1982–83), p. 246.

13. Helen Nebeker, *Woman in Passage: A Critical Study of the Novels of Jean Rhys* (Montréal: Eden Press, 1981).

14. Nancy R. Harrison, *Jean Rhys and the Novel as Women's Text* (Chapel Hill: University of North Carolina Press, 1988).

15. Deborah Kelly Kloepfer, *The Unspeakable Mother: Forbidden Discourse in Jean Rhys and H. D.* (Ithaca, NY: Cornell University Press, 1989).

16. Coral Ann Howells, *Jean Rhys* (New York: Harvester Wheatsheaf, 1991), p. 5.

17. Quoted in Wyndham's introduction to *WSS*, p. 5.

18. Rhys, *Letters 1931–1966*, p. 160.

Chapter 2: *Quartet*: The 'Authored' Woman

1. Rosalind Coward, 'Are Women's Novels Feminist Novels?' in Elaine Showalter (ed.), *The New Feminist Criticism: Essays on Women, Literature and Theory* (London: Virago, 1985), pp. 225–39.

2. Coral Ann Howells, *Jean Rhys* (New York: Harvester Wheatsheaf, 1991), pp. 44–5.

3. Symptomatically enough, it was Ford Madox Ford who gave Jean Rhys, then Ella Lenglet, her pen name. See Jean Rhys, *Letters 1931–1966* (1984; Harmondsworth: Penguin, 1985), p. 65.

4. Susan Gubar, '"The Blank Page" and the Issues of Female Creativity' in Elizabeth Abel (ed.), *Writing and Sexual Difference* (Chicago: University of Chicago Press, 1980), p. 86.

5. Jean Rhys's first novel was published in England as *Postures* and in the USA as *Quartet*. Jean Rhys preferred the American title.

6. Howells, *Jean Rhys*, p. 46.

Chapter 3: *After Leaving Mr Mackenzie*: 'Between Dog and Wolf'

1. Susan Gubar, '"The Blank Page" and the Issues of Female Creativity' in Elizabeth Abel (ed.), *Writing and Sexual Difference* (Chicago: University of Chicago Press, 1980), p. 89.

2. Heterodiegetic: a type of narrator who is absent from the story he tells, who is not part of the cast of characters. See Gérard Genette, *Narrative Discourse: An Essay in Method* (Ithaca, NY: Cornell University Press, 1980), pp. 244–5.

3. Gubar, '"The Blank Page" and the Issues of Female Creativity', p. 80.

4. Translated as 'flat death'. See Roland Barthes, *S/Z* (New York: Hill & Wang, 1974).

5. Diegesis: 'the signified or narrative content' of the story. See Genette, *Narrative Discourse*.

Chapter 4: The Ironic Other

1. Simone de Beauvoir, *The Second Sex* (1949; Harmondsworth: Penguin, 1972).

2. Shoshana Felman, *Diacritics* (1975), quoted in K. K. Ruthven, *Feminist Literary Studies: An Introduction* (Cambridge: Cambridge University Press, 1984), p. 41.

3. Luce Irigaray, *Spéculum de l'autre femme* (Paris: Minuit, 1974).

4. Toril Moi, *Sexual/Textual Politics: Feminist Literary Theory* (1985; London: Routledge 1988), p. 135.

5. Included in *Tigers*, 44–63.

6. Included in *Sleep*, 63–77.

7. Julia Kristeva, *Etrangers à nous-mêmes* (Paris: Gallimard, 1988), pp. 17–18.

8. Included in *Tigers*, 9–36.

9. *Ibid.*, 78–100.

10. Victor Shklovsky, 'Art as Technique' (1917) in Lee T. Lemon and Marion J. Reis (eds), *Russian Formalist Criticism: Four Essays* (Lincoln: University of Nebraska Press, 1965), p. 13.

11. Included in *Tigers*, 37–43.

12. Coral Ann Howells, *Jean Rhys* (New York: Harvester Wheatsheaf, 1991), p. 140.

13. *Ibid.*

14. Included in *Tigers*, 112–28.

15. Linda Hutcheon, *A Theory of Parody: The Teachings of Twentieth-Century Art Forms* (New York: Methuen, 1985), p. 56. By 'ethos', Hutcheon means 'the ruling intended response achieved by a literary text' (*ibid.*, p. 55).

16. *Ibid.*

17. Linda Hutcheon, 'Ironie et parodie: stratégie et structure', *Poétique*, no 36 (1978), p. 475.

18. Hutcheon, *A Theory of Parody*, p. 53.

19. Beda Allemann, 'De l'ironie en tant que principe littéraire', *Poétique*, no. 36 (1978), pp. 390–1.

20. A good friend of hers is called Olly Pearce, a name evocative of the same potentially lethal power.

21. They refer to the logicians' distinction between use and mention: when one *uses* a phrase, one designates what the phrase designates; when one *mentions* a phrase, one designates the phrase itself. See Dan Sperber and Deirdre Wilson, 'Les ironies comme mention', *Poétique*, no. 36 (1978), pp. 399–411.

22. Wayne C. Booth, *A Rhetoric of Irony* (Chicago: University of Chicago Press, 1974), p. 235.

23. *Ibid.*, p. 240.

24. Included in *Tigers*, 64–77.

25. 'I will slay in the day of my Wrath and spare not, saith the Lord God' (*ibid.*, 66).

26. Analepsis: 'any evocation after the fact of an event that took place earlier than the point in the story where we are at any given moment'. See Gérard Genette, *Narrative Discourse: An Essay in Method* (Ithaca, NY: Cornell University Press, 1980), p. 40.

27. Included in *Tigers*, 145–8.

28. *Ibid.*, pp. 101–11.

29. Included in *Sleep*, 43–62.

Chapter 5: *Voyage in the Dark:* 'Two Tunes'

1. Julia Kristeva, 'La femme, ça n'est jamais ça', *Tel Quel*, no. 59 (Fall 1974), translated into English in Elaine Marks and Isabelle de Courtivron (eds), *New French Feminisms* (Brighton: Harvester, 1980), pp. 134–8.

2. Julia Kristeva, *La Révolution du langage poétique* (Paris: Seuil, 1974), translated into English in Toril Moi (ed.), *The Kristeva Reader* (Oxford: Basil Blackwell, 1986), p. 94.

3. *Ibid.*

4. *Ibid.*, p. 96.

5. Toril Moi, *Sexual/Textual Politics: Feminist Literary Theory* (London: Routledge, 1985), p. 162.

6. *Ibid.*

7. Deborah Kelly Kloepfer, *The Unspeakable Mother: Forbidden Discourse in Jean Rhys and H. D.* (Ithaca, NY: Cornell University Press, 1989), p. 63.

8. Nancy R. Harrison, *Jean Rhys and the Novel as Women's Text* (Chapel Hill: University of North Carolina Press, 1988), p. 58.

9. See Jean Rhys, *Letters 1931–1966* (1984; Harmondsworth: Penguin, 1985), p. 149.

10. *Ibid.*, p. 24.

11. Ann Rosalind Jones, 'Writing the body: Toward an Understanding of *l'écriture féminine*' in Elaine Showalter (ed.), *The New Feminist Criticism: Essays on Women, Literature and Theory* (London: Virago, 1985), p. 361.

12. Julia Kristeva, 'About Chinese Women' in Moi (ed.), *The Kristeva Reader*, p. 152.

13. Julia Kristeva, 'Women's Time' in *ibid.*, p. 191.

14. Coral Ann Howells, *Jean Rhys* (New York: Harvester Wheatsheaf, 1991), p. 82.

15. *Ibid.*, p. 70.

16. See *'but we went on dancing forwards and backwards'* (*VD*, 157; my emphasis), *'I thought you'd say that* he *said'* or *'You ought to be going* he *said'* (*VD*, 158; my emphasis). It is through a process of inference only that the reader may find out whom each 'he' refers to. In the case of the pronoun 'we', however, the antecedent remains uncertain.

17. For a discussion of carnival, see in particular Mikhail Bakhtin, *Rabelais and his World* (Bloomington: Indiana University Press, 1984).

18. *Ibid.*, pp. 25–6.

Chapter 6: *Good Morning Midnight*: 'Every Word I Say Has Chains Around its Ankles'

1. Julia Kristeva, *Word, Dialogue and Novel* in Toril Moi (ed.), *The Kristeva Reader* (Oxford: Basil Blackwell, 1986), p. 37.

2. Autodiegetic: a type of narrative 'where the narrator is the hero of his narrative'. See Gérard Genette, *Narrative Discourse: An Essay in Method* (Ithaca, NY: Cornell University Press, 1980), p. 245.

3. In first-person narrative, the final convergence of story time and narrating time is the rule, for a very natural reason, as Gérard Genette explains: the 'length of the story gradually lessens the interval separating it from the moment of the narrating' (*ibid.*, p. 221). *Voyage in the Dark* is open-ended and deletes this final convergence, which reinforces the division between the 'I' whose story is being told and the 'I' who is telling the story.

4. *Ibid.*, p. 218.

5. Mikhail Bakhtin, *The Dialogic Imagination: Four Essays* (Austin: University of Texas Press, 1981), p. 333.

6. *Ibid.*, p. 279.

7. *Ibid.*

8. Philippe Hamon, *Introduction à l'analyse du descriptif* (Paris: Hachette, 1981), p. 52.

9. *Ibid.*, p. 41.

10. *Ibid.*, p. 51.

11. Linda Hutcheon, *A Theory of Parody: The Teachings of Twentieth-Century Art Forms* (New York: Methuen, 1985), p. 33.

12. *Ibid.*, p. 34.

13. *Ibid.*, p. 37.

14. The phrase is Linda Hutcheon's (*ibid.*, p. 41).

15. Antoine Compagnon, *La seconde main ou le travail de la citation* (Paris: Seuil, 1979), p. 23.

16. *Ibid.*, p. 34.

17. Helen Carr, *Jean Rhys* (Plymouth: Northcote House, 1996), p. 80.

18. See *GMM*, pp. 13, 28, 30–1, 34, 159.

19. Quoted in Sandra Gilbert and Susan Gubar, *The Madwoman in the Attic: The Woman Writer and the Nineteenth-Century Literary Imagination* (New Haven: Yale University Press, 1979), p. 46.

Chapter 7: *Wide Sargasso Sea*: The Woman's Text

1. Jean Rhys considered titles as essential components of her books: 'titles mean a lot to me. Almost half the battle' (Jean Rhys, *Letters 1931–1966* [1984; Harmondsworth: Penguin, 1985], p. 154).

2. 'I wrote this book before! – Different setting – same idea. (It was called "Le revenant" then). The MSS was lost [...] – however I discovered two chapters (in another suitcase) and have used them in this book' (*ibid.*, p. 213).

3. Gérard Genette, *Narrative Discourse: An Essay in Method* (Ithaca, NY: Cornell University Press, 1980), p. 67.

4. Tzvetan Todorov, *The Poetics of Prose* (Ithaca, NY: Cornell University Press, 1977), p. 65.

5. Jean Rhys does not give a name to her male narrator, in an attempt perhaps to cloud her indebtedness to Charlotte Brontë. For greater convenience and in order to avoid too many periphrases, I shall call him 'Rochester' with the addition of quotation marks in order to differentiate him from the original character.

6. Genette, *Narrative Discourse*, p. 73.

7. *Ibid.*, p. 75.

8. Coral Ann Howells, *Jean Rhys* (New York: Harvester Wheatsheaf, 1991), p. 110.

9. Rhys, *Letters 1931–1966*, p. 153.

10. Charlotte Brontë, *Jane Eyre* (1847; Harmondsworth: Penguin, 1966), p. 335. All subsequent page numbers refer to this edition.

11. Rhys, *Letters 1931–1966*, p. 161.

12. Harold Bloom, *The Anxiety of Influence: A Theory of Poetry* (Oxford: Oxford University Press, 1973), p. 5.

13. Sandra Gilbert and Susan Gubar, *The Madwoman in the Attic: The Woman Writer and the Nineteenth-Century Literary Imagination* (New Haven: Yale University Press, 1979) *The Anxiety of Influence*, p. 50.

14. *Ibid.*, p. 49.

15. *Ibid.*

16. Bloom, *The Anxiety of Influence*, pp. 15–16.

17. *Ibid.*, p. 141.

18. 'She was a big woman, and had long black hair: we could see it streaming against the flames as she stood' (*Jane Eyre*, 53).

19. Rhys, *Letters 1931–1966*, p. 157.

20. *Ibid.*, p. 156.

21. *Ibid.*, p. 164.

22. *Ibid.*, p. 262.

23. 'The doctors now discovered that *my wife* was mad – her excesses had prematurely developed the germs of insanity' (*Jane Eyre*, 334).

24. See in particular Jane's account of Bertha's visit to her on the eve of her wedding day: 'Sir, it removed my veil from its gaunt head, rent it in two parts, and flinging both on the floor, trampled on them. [...] It drew aside the window-curtain and looked out; perhaps it saw dawn approaching, for, taking the candle, it retreated to the door' (*Jane Eyre*, 311).

25. Michael Thorpe, ' "The Other Side": *Wide Sargasso Sea* and *Jane Eyre*', *Ariel* 8, no. 3 (1977), p. 99.

26. Rhys, *Letters 1931–1966*, p. 156.

27. Donald D. Stone, *The Romantic Impulse in Victorian Fiction* (Cambridge, Mass.: Harvard University Press, 1980), p. 113.

28. Northrop Frye, *Anatomy of Criticism: Four Essays* (Princeton, NJ: Princeton University Press, 1957), p. 187.

29. This is how Gillian Beer designates romantic space: '[t]he enclosed bower, the pleasure dome, the pastoral world, all project images of bliss in which emotional and natural life find repose' (*The Romance* [London: Methuen, 1970], p. 29).

30. Pauline Nestor, *Charlotte Brontë* (Basingstoke: Macmillan ['Women Writers'], 1987), p. 50.

31. Michelle A. Massé, *In the Name of Love: Women, Masochism and the Gothic* (Ithaca, NY: Cornell University Press, 1992), p. 231.

32. *Ibid.*, p. 208.

33. Gilbert and Gubar, *The Madwoman in the Attic*, p. 338.

34. Frye, *Anatomy of Criticism*.

35. Working on the assumption that Gothic fiction presents masochism as an element of women's identity, Michelle A. Massé uses Freud's 'beating fantasy', psychoanalysis's most thorough exploration of the issue, to demonstrate that, far from being self-inflicted, masochism is a social script women are taught to live out. In *Jane Eyre*, she argues, Jane puts an end to the Gothic beating fantasy by refusing to assign 'her identity to another' and to conflate 'the self-chosen limits of love and the other-imposed restraints of authority' (Massé, *In the Name of Love*, p. 231).

36. Robert B. Heilman, 'Charlotte Brontë's "New" Gothic' in Ian Gregor (ed.), *The Brontës: A Collection of Critical Essays* (Englewood Cliffs, NJ: Prentice Hall, 1970), p. 98.

37. *Ibid.*

38. Stone, *The Romantic Impulse in Victorian Fiction*, p. 116.

39. Gilbert and Gubar, *The Madwoman in the Attic*, p. 360.

40. Tzvetan Todorov, *The Fantastic: A Structural Approach to a Literary Genre* (London: Case Western Reserve University Press, 1973).

41. Rhys, *Letters 1931–1966*, p. 268.

42. Beer, *The Romance*, p. 2.

43. Northrop Frye, *The Secular Scripture: A Study of the Structure of Romance* (Cambridge, Mass.: Harvard University Press, 1976), p. 53.

44. Fredric Jameson, 'Magical Narratives: Romance as Genre', *New Literary History*, 7, no. 1 (Autumn 1975), p. 158.

45. Gérard Genette, *Figures II* (Paris: Seuil, 1969), pp. 96–7.

46. Todorov, *The Fantastic*.

47. Anthony Luengo, '*Wide Sargasso Sea* and the Gothic Mode', *World Literature Written in English*, no. 15 (April 1976), p. 235.

48. *Ibid.*, p. 232.

49. *Ibid.*, p. 235.

50. *Ibid.*, p. 242.

51. Rosemary Jackson, *Fantasy: The Literature of Subversion* (London: Routledge, 1981), p. 97.

52. *Ibid.*, p. 25.

53. *Ibid.*, p. 26.

54. *Ibid.*, p. 38.

55. *Ibid.*, p. 29.

56. *Ibid.*, p. 40.

57. Helen Carr, *Jean Rhys* (Plymouth: Northcote House, 1996), p. 77.

58. Jackson, *Fantasy*, p. 48.

59. *Ibid.*, p. 84.

60. *Ibid.*, p. 21.

61. Nancy R. Harrison, *Jean Rhys and the Novel as Women's Text* (Chapel Hill: University of North Carolina Press, 1988), p. 252.

62. Shoshana Felman, *La Folie et la chose littéraire* (Paris: Seuil, 1978), p. 148.

63. Shoshana Felman defines the woman's problem as follows: 'comment se défaire de cette imposition (culturelle) de folie, sans pour autant assumer les positions critiques et thérapeutiques de la raison? comment éviter de parler tout à la fois en tant que *folle* et en tant que *non folle*?' (*ibid.*, pp. 154–5; 'how can a woman undo this (cultural) imposition of madness, while not assuming the critical and therapeutical positions of reason? How can she avoid speaking either as a mad woman or as an un-mad one?' [my translation]).

64. Harrison, *Jean Rhys*, p. 122.

Bibliography

Works by Jean Rhys

The Left Bank and Other Stories (London: Jonathan Cape, 1927).
Quartet (1928; Harmondsworth: Penguin, 1973).
After Leaving Mr Mackenzie (1930; Harmondsworth: Penguin, 1971).
Voyage in the Dark (1934; Harmondsworth: Penguin, 1969).
Good Morning Midnight (1939; Harmondsworth: Penguin, 1969).
Wide Sargasso Sea (1966; Harmondsworth: Penguin, 1968).
Tigers Are Better-Looking (1968; Harmondsworth: Penguin, 1972).
My Day (New York: Frank Hallman, 1975).
Sleep It Off Lady (1976; Harmondsworth: Penguin, 1979).
Smile Please (1979; Harmondsworth: Penguin, 1981).
Letters 1931–1966 (1984; Harmondsworth: Penguin, 1985, selected and edited by Francis Wyndham and Diana Melly).

Selected Works About Jean Rhys

Angier, Carole, *Jean Rhys: Life and Work* (London: André Deutsch, 1990).
Carr, Helen, *Jean Rhys* (Plymouth: Northcote House, 1996).
Delourme, Chantal, 'La mémoire fécondée. Réflexions sur l'intertextualité: *Jane Eyre, Wide Sargasso Sea*', *Etudes anglaises*, no. 3 (juillet–septembre 1989), pp. 257–69.
—— 'La citation-méduse dans *Good Morning Midnight*', *Les années 30*, no. 14 (juin 1991), pp. 45–57.
Harrison, Nancy R., *Jean Rhys and the Novel as Women's Text* (Chapel Hill: University of North Carolina Press, 1988).
Howells, Coral Ann, *Jean Rhys* (New York: Harvester Wheatsheaf, 1991).
Joubert, Claire, *Lire le féminin: Dorothy Richardson, Katherine Mansfield, Jean Rhys* (Paris: Messene, 1997).
Kegan Gardiner, Judith, '*Good Morning Midnight*, Good Night Modernism', *Boundary 2*, no. 1–2, vol. 11 (1982–83).
Kloepfer, Deborah Kelly, *The Unspeakable Mother: Forbidden Discourse in Jean Rhys and H. D.* (Ithaca, NY: Cornell University Press, 1989).
Le Gallez, Paula, *The Rhys Woman* (Basingstoke: Macmillan, 1990).
Look Lai, Wally, 'The Road to Thornfield Hall: A Review of *Wide Sargasso Sea*', *New Beacon Reviews* (1968).
Luengo, Anthony, '*Wide Sargasso Sea* and the Gothic Mode', *World Literature Written in English*, no. 15 (April 1976).

Maurel, Sylvie, 'L'autoportrait ou le tombeau de Narcisse dans *Smile Please* de Jean Rhys', *Jean Rhys Review*, no. 2, vol. 4 (1990), pp. 12–19.

Mellown, Elgin W., *Jean Rhys: A Descriptive and Annotated Bibliography of Works and Criticism* (New York: Garland Publishing Inc., 1984).

Mills, S., L. Pearce, S. Spaull and E. Millard, *Feminist Readings/Feminists Reading* (New York: Harvester Wheatsheaf, 1989).

Nebeker, Helen, *Woman in Passage: A Critical Study of the Novels of Jean Rhys* (Montréal: Eden Press, 1981).

O'Connor, Teresa, *Jean Rhys: The West Indian Novels* (New York: New York University Press, 1986).

Ramchand, Kenneth, *The West Indian Novel and its Background* (1970; London: Heinemann, 1983).

Staley, Thomas F., *Jean Rhys: A Critical Study* (London: Macmillan, 1979).

Thorpe, Michael, ' "The Other Side": *Wide Sargasso Sea* and *Jane Eyre*', *Ariel*, 8, no. 3 (1977).

Other Works Mentioned in the Text

Abel, Elizabeth (ed.), *Writing and Sexual Difference* (Chicago: University of Chicago Press, 1980).

Allemann, Beda, 'De l'ironie en tant que principe littéraire', *Poétique*, no. 36 (1978).

Bakhtin, Mikhail, *The Dialogic Imagination: Four Essays* (edited by Michael Holquist and translated by Caryl Emerson and Michael Holquist, Austin: University of Texas Press, 1981).

—— *Rabelais and his World* (translated by Helene Iswolsky, Bloomington: Indiana University Press, 1984).

Barthes, Roland, *S/Z* (translated by Richard Miller, New York: Hill & Wang, 1974).

Beer, Gillian, *The Romance* (London: Methuen, 1970).

Bloom, Harold, *The Anxiety of Influence: A Theory of Poetry* (Oxford: Oxford University Press, 1973).

Booth, Wayne C., *A Rhetoric of Irony* (Chicago: University of Chicago Press, 1974).

Brontë, Charlotte, *Jane Eyre* (1847; Harmondsworth: Penguin, 1966).

Compagnon, Antoine, *La seconde Main ou le travail de la citation* (Paris: Seuil, 1979).

de Beauvoir, Simone, *The Second Sex* (1949; Harmondsworth: Penguin, 1972).

Felman, Shoshana, *La Folie et la chose littéraire* (Paris: Seuil, 1978).

Frye, Northrop, *Anatomy of Criticism: Four Essays* (Princeton, NJ: Princeton University Press, 1957).

—— *The Secular Scripture: A Study of the Structure of Romance* (Cambridge, Mass.: Harvard University Press, 1976).

Genette, Gérard, *Figures II* (Paris: Seuil, 1969).

—— *Narrative Discourse: An Essay in Method* (Ithaca, NY: Cornell University Press, 1980).

Gilbert, Sandra and Susan Gubar, *The Madwoman in the Attic: The Woman Writer and the Nineteenth-Century Literary Imagination* (New Haven: Yale University Press, 1979).

Hamon, Philippe, *Introduction à l'analyse du descriptif* (Paris: Hachette, 1981).

Heilman, Robert B., 'Charlotte Brontë's "New" Gothic' in Ian Gregor (ed.), *The Brontës: A Collection of Critical Essays* (Englewood Cliffs, NJ: Prentice Hall, 1970).

Hutcheon, Linda, 'Ironie et parodie: stratégie et structure', *Poétique*, no. 36 (1978).

—— *A Theory of Parody: The Teachings of Twentieth-Century Art Forms* (New York: Methuen, 1985).

Irigaray, Luce, *Spéculum de l'autre femme* (Paris: Minuit, 1974).

Jackson, Rosemary, *Fantasy: The Literature of Subversion* (London: Routledge, 1981).

Jameson, Fredric, 'Magical Narratives: Romance as Genre', *New Literary History*, 7, no. 1 (Autumn 1975), pp. 135–63.

Kristeva, Julia, *Etrangers à nous-mêmes* (Paris: Gallimard, 1988).

Marks, Elaine and Isabelle de Courtivron (eds), *New French Feminisms* (Brighton: Harvester, 1980).

Massé, Michelle A., *In the Name of Love: Women, Masochism and the Gothic* (Ithaca, NY: Cornell University Press, 1992).

Moi, Toril, *Sexual/Textual Politics: Feminist Literary Theory* (1985; London: Routledge, 1988).

Moi, Toril (ed.), *The Kristeva Reader* (Oxford: Basil Blackwell, 1986).

Nestor, Pauline, *Charlotte Brontë* (Basingstoke: Macmillan ['Women Writers'], 1987).

Ruthven, K. K., *Feminist Literary Studies: An Introduction* (Cambridge: Cambridge University Press, 1984).

Shklovsky, Victor, 'Art as Technique' (1917) in Lee T. Lemon and Marion J. Reis (eds), *Russian Formalist Criticism: Four Essays* (Lincoln: University of Nebraska Press, 1965).

Showalter, Elaine, *A Literature of Their Own: British Women Novelists from Brontë to Lessing* (Princeton, NJ: Princeton University Press, 1977).

Showalter, Elaine (ed.), *The New Feminist Criticism: Essays on Women, Literature and Theory* (London: Virago, 1985).

Sperber, Dan and Deirdre Wilson, 'Les ironies comme mention', *Poétique*, no. 36 (1978).

Stone, Donald D., *The Romantic Impulse in Victorian Fiction* (Cambridge, Mass.: Harvard University Press, 1980).

Todorov, Tzvetan, *The Fantastic: A Structural Approach to a Literary Genre* (translated by Richard Howard, London: Case Western Reserve University Press, 1973).

—— *The Poetics of Prose* (Ithaca, NY: Cornell University Press, 1977).

Index